open

D1743008

open

open

editorial

JORINDE SEIJDEL

TRANSPARENCY
PUBLICITY AND SECRECY IN THE AGE
OF WIKILEAKS

Taking WikiLeaks as an illustrative example, *Open* 22 investigates how transparency and secrecy relate to one another, to the public and to publicity in our computerized visual cultures. This issue continues to explore what for *Open* are fundamental themes such as privatization, mediatization and the demand for the communal. In the more general sense, it examines transparency as an ideology, the ideal of the free flow of information versus the fight over access to information and the intrinsic connection between publicity and secrecy. It also tries to come to grips with the social and political implications of the phenomenon of WikiLeaks, which, with the illustrious Julian Assange as front man, produces an effect on a global scale. While most people would agree that WikiLeaks has started something that is unstoppable; there is hardly any consensus on its morality, effectiveness or strategy, neither in conservative nor in progressive circles.

WikiLeaks, as the counterpart of the 'transparent' citizen or consumer, expresses a growing public desire for openness and transparency as regards the state, businesses and administrators – a demand for publicity that is continually fed by floods of sensational social and political revelations. And whereas people often consider secrecy within the public sphere to be inadmissible and clandestine, transparency is associated with democracy, participation and accessibility. But does transparency only work in a liberating way? Can it not equally have a concealing or controlling effect? Aren't certain forms of transparency actually the manifestation of the banality of the contemporary spectacle, which revolves around pure display and the production of affects?

In any case, with their capacity to immediately reproduce and disseminate information, the media play a crucial role in the social process of displaying and disclosing. But on behalf of whom are they doing this, and for whom? Do they not increasingly form an abstract power?

Two introductory essays explore political and social notions of transparency and secrecy. Media theorist Felix Stalder searches for a form of transparency that is not employed as a means of power and control, such as in neoliberal market thinking, but that can express and strengthen social solidarity. Stefan Nowotny, philosopher, goes into publicity and openness as a modern myth in relation to the production of affects and the exercise of power, and finds that secrecy and publicity are intertwined more than ever.

Other pieces directly examine WikiLeaks and its implications. Philosopher and media theorist Boris Groys argues that WikiLeaks' democratic universal openness is based on the most absolute secretiveness, and as a matter of fact is a conspiracy. The American political theorist Jodi Dean shows herself to be extremely critical about WikiLeaks, stating that too much information is a greater handicap than too little information in 'communicative capitalism' and that Julian Assange, by becoming a star in his own story, takes attention away from the political issues he says he wants to bring to the public's attention. The interview conducted by Willem van Weelden, researcher-publicist on interactive media, with media theorist Geert Lovink and political scientist/sociologist Merijn Oudenampsen goes into the question of whether and how WikiLeaks brings about social and political change, and what the platform means for contemporary forms of art and activism. In the column, Jorinde Seijdel wonders where WikiLeaks and Facebook converge, seeing as both avow transparency as their ideology but apparently out of very different motives.

Transparency and secrecy are also relevant concepts in art and architecture. The art historian Roel Griffioen posits that, analogous to social developments, the ideal of the glass house in modern and contemporary architecture has made way for the house of one-way glass, in which concealing has become just as important as displaying. Art theorist Sven Lütticken discusses how the structure of the modern art work offers the perfect means of gaining insight into the dialectics of opacity and transparency in this age of public secrets. The work of Amsterdam-based American artist Zachary Formwalt, who also made a special visual contribution to this issue, is one example of this.

This issue features a number of excerpts from *Failed States*, a manuscript-in-progress by American artist Jill Magid that investigates transparency and secrecy out of Magid's desire to be an eyewitness to the 'war on terror' and the media's representation of it. British artist Heath Bunting contributed a fold-out flowchart that explores the porous borders between the individual, their 'data body' and corporations.

Illustrations of a project by designer Floor Koomen and graphic design students of the Rietveld Academie in Amsterdam can be found throughout this issue. The assignment consisted of selecting a leak from the WikiLeaks website and editing and designing it for a print-on-demand publication, thus providing us with a critical look at WikiLeaks as a medium and the current position of journalism.
(see: www.orderyourwikileak.org/)

Felix Stalder

The Fight over Transparency

From a Hierarchical to a Horizontal Organization

Media theorist Felix Stalder describes the changed agenda of transparency in today's neo-liberal era. That agenda's regime of measurability and standardization leads people to make forced choices in order not to be isolated or excluded. In order to avoid this, a new form of transparency is necessary, one that is horizontally organized and employs the newest means of communication.

Two radically different transparency paradigms are operating simultaneously. Within liberal political theory, the demand for transparency is directed at state institutions to create accountability to the public, that is to say the citizens from whom they derive their legitimacy. Within neoliberal political theory, the demand for transparency is directed at market participants to reduce uncertainty within a globalized sphere of action and abstraction. On the one hand, there is the question of how old notions of transparency can be made to function again within the context of a complex information society. WikiLeaks is currently the most effective actor in this debate. On the other hand, as market logic has expanded across nearly all domains of life and turns increasingly repressive as the economic crisis evolves, a different critique of transparency has been formulated, emphasizing subversive strategies of *in*transparency and a refusal to become visible and accessible. To understand the political dynamics of transparency more comprehensively – as both empowerment and control – we must look at all forms of transparency in terms of the social relationships they produce.

Accountability

Transparency – the accessibility of records of the internal processes of public institutions to third parties – is a key element of the functioning of the institutional system of checks and balances. One branch of government can meaningfully control the other and a flourishing public sphere can be created, so that elected officials (and the civil servants they oversee) can be held to account by their constituencies. For Max Weber, one of the defining characteristic of modern 'legal authority' is that 'acts, decisions, and rules are formulated and recorded in writing, even in cases where oral discussion is the rule or is even mandatory [in court, for instance]. This applies at least to preliminary discussions and proposals, to final decisions, and to all sorts of orders and rules'.[1] How many of these records are actually publicly accessible and hence really contribute to transparency through the public sphere is of course a matter of contestation and varies according to the balance of power imbedded in state institutions. Roughly speaking, however, through mechanisms such as Freedom of Information (FOI) legislation, which gives citizens the right to demand the release of records, the basic model established in the nineteenth century – requiring public institutions to record their actions and to grant access to these records – has steadily been expanded in Western countries. At the same time, there is a growing perception that many public institutions have nevertheless become

1. Max Weber, *Economy and Society* (1922), translated by Guenther Roth and Claus Wittich (New York: Bedminster Press, 1968), 219.

less transparent and that the gulf between the state and its citizens has widened. Democracy is slipping into a veritable crisis of legitimacy.[2] In part, this crisis stems from the inadequacy of the means that are supposed to create transparency. There are structural and political reasons for this. First, getting access to the records is cumbersome. For example, submitting a Freedom of Information request can be very complicated, and the response subsequently takes months. In the end, moreover, any request can be denied for opaque reasons. Second, the complexity of government and the mass of records have grown so much that it is increasingly difficult to determine in advance which individual records are relevant and thus warrant a FOI request. Often, what provides genuine insight is not an individual record, but a large body of records viewed together. Yet the format of the records (often paper records, or if electronic, handed over as printouts) makes it very difficult to process them in the quantities required to understand complex procedures. There is also a subjective aspect to this. In an age in which we have grown accustomed to instant access to masses of information through sophisticated infrastructures, the slowness and complexity of these official processes seem like acts of obstruction. There is, in other words, a mismatch between

2. Colin Crouch, *Post-Democracy* (Cambridge: Polity Press, 2004).

the means available in practice and the ends these means should achieve in theory, even if the system were to work without obstruction within its current design. But it does not, since there is also a political side to the problem. Public officials have found it convenient to shield more and more of their activities from public scrutiny – particularly those they fear will generate critical reactions from the public. They do so by invoking the catch-all spectre of national security, by interpreting notions of 'executive privilege' very broadly, or simply by adopting secrecy as a mode of operation, particularly in international negotiations. For instance, the Anti-Counterfeiting Trade Agreement (ACTA), a controversial but by and large standard treaty, was negotiated in secret for two years before the existence of negotiations was even publicly confirmed. Even then, it took another two years and a massive public campaign before the near-final draft was officially released in April 2010. As Michael Geist concluded, 'it represent[ed] a major shift toward greater secrecy . . . in an obvious attempt to avoid public participation and scrutiny.'[3] The combined effect of these structural and political dynamics is that the state is seen as neither capable nor willing to provide transpar-

3. Michael Geist, 'ACTA Guide, Part Three: Transparency and ACTA Secrecy', *Michael Geist's Blog* (michaelgeist.ca), 27 January 2010: http://www.michaelgeist.ca/content/view/4737/125/ (last accessed on 15 July 2011).

ency in a manner adequate to generating democratic debates about central aspects of its activities.

The Role of WikiLeaks

WikiLeaks aims to intervene on both levels. First by providing access to public records in ways that are adequate to the technological culture of the present. They are put online, made searchable and machine-readable, downloadable, and are available to anyone, for any purpose, without registration or other access controls. Second by providing access to records of public interest that have been shielded from the public, even in the face of explicit FOI requests. The case in point is the video of an Apache helicopter whose pilots shot a group of unarmed men, including journalists Saeed Chmagh and Namir Noor-Eldeen, in Baghdad on 12 July 2007. The journalists' employer at the time, Reuters, immediately filed a FOI request for this video, but this request was repeatedly denied. On 5 April 2010, WikiLeaks released this video under the title *Collateral Murder*, in an edited and an unedited version. Once the video was released, it became clear that the FOI request had been denied primarily because the video was highly embarrassing to the US government.

Despite the controversy about and hostility against WikiLeaks stirred up by angry officials and envious media, as well as considerable tensions and contradictions inside the project itself,[4] the public response to the releases has been overwhelmingly positive. Its editor in chief, Julian Assange, has become a global celebrity and a hero to many. WikiLeaks can rely on a widespread sentiment that public institutions are not transparent enough and that unconventional means of providing transparency are necessary. This sentiment was latent before WikiLeaks came into being, but the project has brought it to the fore and at the same time radicalized demand for new forms of transparency. While WikiLeaks itself is currently somewhat in limbo (it has not accepted new submissions since late 2010), the dynamics it accelerated are now propelling other initiatives forward. On the one hand, existing initiatives that seek to renew the official mechanisms for generating transparency have received a boost and new ones are springing up. For example, government open-data initiatives have been created all over the world over the last year or two. The idea here is that instead of granting access to individual (paper) records, governments should provide access to entire databases in open and machine-readable formats over the Internet, so that third parties can take and interpret this data in any way they see fit. There is now a serious debate on the type of data-

4. Daniel Domscheit-Berg, *Inside WikiLeaks: My Time with Julian Assange at the World's Most Dangerous Website* (New York: Random House, 2011).

Knowbotic, *MacGhillie, just a void*, 2008-2010.
Photo Christoph Oeschger

The Fight over Transparency

Knowbotic, *MacGhillie, just a void*, 2008-2010.
Photo Christoph Oeschger

bases that can or need to be made accessible in this way, and the technological standards that define how the data can accessed and used.

A number of new laws, either just passed or currently in preparation, aim to increase the transparency of politics, particularly in relation to the flow of money from lobbyists and the financing of political parties. On the other hand, heavy-handed attempts to cripple WikiLeaks by leaning on key providers of communications infrastructure – payment networks, cloud computing services or domain name registrars – have politicized and radicalized a new generation of hackers. These share none of the concerns of WikiLeaks about the ethics and responsibilities of independent publishing (however idiosyncratically Wiki-Leaks may have interpreted these in practice). Rather than wait for whistle-blowers, they break into systems to gather data, and rather than edit the material to protect individuals and provide context, they simply dump the raw material on the Internet. All of this has prompted a wide-ranging debate about the legitimacy of secrecy for public institutions and the need to find better ways of ensuring that transparency, in practical terms, can continue to fulfil its function within the liberal conception of the state.

Assumptions

This revival of the liberal notion of transparency warrants a revival of its critique. Henry Lefebvre's analysis, formulated in the early 1970s, is now more relevant than ever: 'The presumption [behind the demands for transparency] is that an encrypted reality becomes readily decipherable thanks to the intervention of first speech and then of writing . . . In any event, the spoken and written word are taken for (social) practices, it is assumed that absurdity and obscurity, which are treated as aspects of the same thing, may be dissipated without any corresponding disappearance of the 'object'... Such are the assumptions of an ideology which, in positing the transparency of space, identifies knowledge, information and communication. It was on the basis of this ideology that people believed for quite a time that revolutionary social change could be achieved by means of communication alone.'[5]

5. Henri Lefebvre, *The Production of Space* (1974), translated by Donald Nicholson-Smith (Oxford: Black-well, 1991), 28-29.

Underlying the *ideology of transparency* Lefebvre identified is the assumption that it is primarily the lack of communication and knowledge that prevents institutions from functioning properly, and, conversely, that more communication and more knowledge will, by themselves, correct this problem. This assumption was as problematic in 1974 as it is now. In Lefebvre's view (and that of other Marxists), the main issue regarding the operations of state institutions was not their inefficiency, but the antagonistic social relationships they embodied. Making the state work more efficiently by increasing transparency would solve only the bourgeoisie's problems. Radical politics, on the other hand, would have to change the social relationships embodied in and reproduced by the state. Current critics of open-data initiatives, few as they are, see related issues, although they follow an analysis of power more in line with Pierre Bourdieu's. Michael Gurstein, for example, focuses on the cultural specificity of information released by open-data initiatives and the patterns of inclusion and exclusion they (re) produce. Analysing the transparency site for parliaments in the UK (TheyWorkForYou.com), one of the more prominent open-data projects to date, he concludes that 'this attempt to enhance democratic participation has ended up providing an additional opportunity for those who . . . because of their income, education, and overall conventional characteristics of higher status (age, gender, etc.) already have the means to communicate with and influence politicians. The additional information and an additional communications channel thus [have] the effect of reinforcing patterns of opportunity that are already there rather than widening the base of participation and influence.'[6]

His critique serves as a warning against the assumed objectivity (aka 'the data speaks for itself') and capacity of transparency to bypass murky politics. He points out that the production of knowledge itself is already political, and that providing transparency is not the end, but just another step in the long march of politics.

Control

This part of the debate can be understood as an upgrading of the nineteenth-century transparency paradigm to the twenty-first century. In the meantime, however, a very different analysis of transparency has been proposed, most notably by the Tiqqun collective[7] and by Brian Holmes.[8] They take as their starting point cybernetic capitalism and neoliberalism, developed after the Second World War and having gained social dominance as the answer to the crisis of Keynesian industrial capitalism in the 1970s. In this

6. Michael Gurstein, 'Are the Open Data Warriors Fighting for Robin Hood or the Sheriff?: Some Reflections on OKCon 2011 and the Emerging Data Divide', *Gurstein's Community Informatics* (gurstein.wordpress.com), 3 July 2011: http://wp.me/pJQl5-79 (last accessed on 15 July 2011).

7. Tiqqun, 'The Cybernetic Hypothesis', *Tiqqun* no. 2, 2001, English translation posted on http://cybernet.jottit.com/ in 2009 (last accessed on 15 July 2011). (See also: http://theanarchistlibrary.org/HTML/Tiqqun__The_Cybernetic_Hypothesis.html)

8. Brian Holmes, 'Future Map', *Continental Drift* (brianholmes.wordpress.com), 9 September 2007: http://brianholmes.wordpress.com/2007/09/09/future-map/.

process a very different notion of transparency was established. Instead of being concerned with the accountability of public institutions towards citizens, it was conceived as a way to reduce 'information asymmetries'. Its main function, therefore, was to make markets work more efficiently. This concern with the role of information in the functioning of markets stems from the idea of markets as being composed of highly decentralized actors operating locally but coordinating across space with one another through the market.

This perspective was famously formulated by F.A. Hayek right at the end of the Second World War. For him, there are two types of information. One is the actor's 'limited but intimate knowledge of the facts of his immediate surroundings'; the other is provided by the 'price system as . . . a system of telecommunications which enables individual producers to watch merely the movement of a few pointers, as an engineer might watch the hands of a few dials'.[9]

For this system to work properly, agents need as much informa-

9. Friedrich A. Hayek, 'The Use of Knowledge in Society', *American Economic Review*, vol. 35, no. 4 (September 1945), 519-530.

tion as possible about their 'immediate surroundings' and the price mechanism must not be distorted by regulatory interventions in the markets. To advance this vision in a globalizing world, two problems need to be addressed. One is that gaining knowledge of one's 'imme-

diate surroundings' becomes problematic, due to the loss of intimate connections to one's physical surrounding through the destruction of local social bonds. At the same time, one's 'immediate' surroundings have expanded to the point where they encompass the entire planet. This is yet another instance of Marshall McLuhan's famous global village. The other problem is that for the markets to work in this fashion, they need to become integrated globally. In this perspective, national borders are viewed as market-distorting mechanisms.

One way of understanding globalization, therefore, is as a process of standardization[10] aimed at addressing these two issues, which according to this theory prevent

10. David Singh Grewal, *Network Power: The Social Dynamics of Globalization* (New Haven/London: Yale University Press, 2008).

markets from functioning properly. The latter issue is addressed by the World Trade Organization (WTO) and various bilateral or multilateral free-trade agreements, the former through the development of diverse 'transparency regimes' defined as government mandates that require corporations or other organizations to provide the public with factual information about their products and practices. Disclosed information is structured for comparability and updated at regular intervals.[11]

11. Archon Fung, Mary Graham, David Weil and Elena Fagotto, *The Political Economy of Transparency: What Makes Disclosure Policies Effective?* (December 2004), research paper available at Social Science Research Network (SSRN): http://ssrn.com/abstract=766287 (last accessed on 15 July 2011).

Because of the fracturing of social space locally as well as the problem of global integration, transparency regimes have been implemented on every scale. A local example would be Los Angeles County's restaurant grading system, adopted in 1997, which requires restaurants to prominently display the results of their most recent hygiene inspection, expressed in grades of A, B or C. Consumers can now see which establishments passed their most recent inspections and factor this into their purchase decisions. Global examples are equally ubiquitous, ranging from reporting requirements for publicly traded companies to the standardized statistical reporting of entire national economies. The increasing importance of institutions such as the International Standards Organization (ISO) and their expansion from the standardizing of objects to the standardizing of processes, quality management in particular (through the ISO 9000 standards), is a testament to this development.

The operative words here are expansion and standards. While the dream of cybernetics to create a new meta-science failed to materialize and lost its attraction in the 1960s, its fusion with free-market ideology proved very potent. Over the last 30 years, virtually every aspect of social life has been made measurable, standardized, comparable, and then linked to some form of financial marker, be it price, debt or a budget item. The whole of society has been made to function according to cybernetic market principles, and the process engineers of management can now monitor everything simply by tracking a few numbers.

Standardization Leads to Forced Choices

Creating transparency has been a crucial step in this process. If we recall the value that Hayek placed on the economic actor's need for intimate knowledge of his 'immediate surroundings' and that the role of transparency is to increase that knowledge, it is hardly surprising that the social consequences of this evolution have been highly uneven. They favour those who can act most effectively through the market while subjecting everyone else to ever more stringent disciplinary regimes. That is the expansion part. Subjugation to this new regime has not been achieved through force, at least not primarily. It has been achieved through the establishment of particular standards capable of unleashing these dynamics.

A standard constitutes 'the particular way in which a group of people is interconnected in a network. It is the shared norm or practice that enables network members to gain access to one another, facilitating their cooperation'.[12] As such, standards seem

12. Grewal, *Network Power*, op. cit. (note 10), 21.

rather innocent; indeed, they are indispensable in coordinating the interaction of formally independent agents. However, they set the rules by which these agents can interact. Once a standard has been established, it can constitute an 'all-or-nothing' proposition. The standard must be accepted in order to gain access to a particular network and the resources and opportunities present within it. If the standard is not accepted, there is no access. From the point of view of the outsider, adopting a particular standard can seem a forced choice, since the alternative would be social isolation; from the point of view of the network, standard acceptance is always voluntary.

The case in point is the WTO. It is the enforcer of the neoliberal empire on a global scale. Yet this is clearly not gunboat imperialism: the WTO is a voluntary organization to which nation-states have to apply for membership. The result is structural coercion under conditions of formal freedom.[13] Entire states, organiza-   13. See ibid.
tions large and small, and individual people voluntarily submit to coercive regimes because these constitute the conditions under which they can gain access to particular resources and opportunities. No matter how rigged the game might be, in a networked age, isolation would almost always be worse. Think of applying for a grant for a cultural project or joining Facebook. You hate it, but you still agree to it, while pretending to like it.

Because there is (normally) no direct coercion forcing people into a particular standard, but rather individual voluntary decisions to adopt it, power is dispersed and difficult to localize. The appropriate way to confront this type of power is therefore not to attack the holders of power, but to challenge the particular standard through which it operates. Tiqqun, however, outlined a more radical approach. Instead of confronting a particular standard, it aims to subvert the underlying mode of operation of an entire class of standards – those identified as part of the cybernetic control regime. This underlying mode of operation is the creation of transparency. Consequently, Tiqqun developed a set of tactics to reduce transparency, thus undermining a key operating requirement for these standards. The key tactic proposed is to become invisible, to withdraw from the action (as a strategic retreat, not as an escapist fantasy) – to turn into fog: 'Fog is a vital response to the imperative of clarity, transparency, which is the first imprint of imperial power on bodies. To become foglike means that I finally take up the part of the shadows that command me and prevent me from believing all the fictions of direct democracy insofar as they intend to ritualize the transparency of each person in their own interests, and of all persons in the interests of all. To become opaque like fog means recognizing that we don't represent anything, that we aren't identifiable; it means taking on the untotalizable character of the physical body as a political body; it means opening yourself up to still-unknown possibilities. It means resisting with all your power any struggle for recognition.'[14]

This approach has been enormously influential and particularly productive in the arts, where there has been a string of recent projects (like Andreas Broeckmann & Knowbotic Research's 2010 *Opaque Presence*[15] or Seth Price's 2008 *How to Disappear in America*)[16] and exhibitions (like HMKV's 'Gone to Croatan', 2011)[17] dealing with invisibility, disappearance and forms of withdrawal. This strong interest from artists is perhaps not surprising, as Tiqqun formulates not so much a political as an aesthetic strategy (fog, invisibility, opacity, rhythm, slowness, and so forth). In scale, the approach is individualisitic (even if Tiqqun speaks of small collectives) and in sentiment it is Romantic (reclaiming spontaneous life against the

14. Tiqqun, 'The Cybernetic Hypothesis', op. cit. (note 7).

15. Andreas Broeckmann and Knowbotic Research (eds.), *Opaque Presence: Manual of Latent Invisibilities* (Berlin/Zurich: Diaphanes/ Éditions Jardins des Pilotes, 2010).

16. Seth Price, *How to Disappear in America* (New York: The Leopard Press, 2008).

17. 'Gone to Croatan – Strategien des Verschwindens', group exibition by Hartware Medienkunstverein (HMKV), Dortmunder U, Dortmund, Germany, 4 June-14 August 2011.

dead hand of control) making it well suited to artistic practices, but problematic for a wider politics.

Horizontally Organized Transparency

The inversion of the critique of transparency into a politics of invisibility leads to a dead end of romanticizing clandestine groups whose internal communications intensity must compensate for a lack of external connections. It ends up sacrificing the one key contemporary innovation that can make new forms of political agency possible: the ease with which new 'weak' connections can be generated through digital media, enabling the synchronization of independent agencies into a new collective rhythm. This synchronization is enabled through small acts of trust – which may lead to greater acts of trust further down the road – made possible through particular forms of visibility. People come to see one another and experience zones of mutuality (and zones of conflicts). For this, some sort of transparency is absolutely crucial. Without the recognition of a mutuality of affects, social solidarity cannot emerge. And without relatively open forms of transparency, mutuality cannot increase in scale, remaining locked in a fractured landscape of small communities that communicate with one another through clandestine channels invisible to outsiders. In other words, intensity is no substitute for scale.

We must differentiate between different modes of transparency and the social relationships they enable. Transparency within the liberal conception, in its nineteenth- and twenty-first-century forms, takes the existence of hierarchical state institutions and of power through representation as a given, but aims to balance it with what one might call 'bottom-up' visibility. Because it recognizes that the state is based on a design in which institutions concentrate power, it needs mechanisms to hold those inside these institutions – that is, those who hold power – accountable to those outside whom they are supposed to serve These relationships of accountability should not be casually dismissed, but they no longer suffice, because power no longer operates merely through institutions but increasingly through standards. These currently dominant standards demand particular forms of transparency that, in effect, create a kind of 'top-down' visibility, whereby those with substantial information-processing capacities can adjust, more or less subtly and to their own benefit, the conditions under which all others operate as 'free agents'. Rather than work through commands, power operates through the seemingly neutral formulation of 'if . . . then' propositions. The transparency of the social body ensures that these propositions are subtle enough to be read as statements of facts, rather than as acts of coercion.

If we accept that standards are ways to enable the social coordination of autonomous agents (that is, those outside hierarchical command-and-obey structures) we need to develop different standards that are not infused by the neoliberal programme. If we accept that contemporary sociality needs to operate on a global scale, we need to find ways of articulating mutuality on that scale. A precondition of this is a form of visibility that allows for the synchronization of actions without feeding the machine of cybernetic control. Thus, we need a paradigm of transparency that is strictly horizontal, that enables us to extend sociality to a very large scale. This requires new standards of communication, new tools of communication that actively support the experience of mutuality and actively prevent the implementation of top-down visibility.

Exclusivity Period Conditions. During the Market Exclusivity Period, Licensor shall not license any Immersive Imagery Data (whether accepted or rejected by Google), or any other Licensor street-level imagery (whether or not geo-referenced) to any Prohibited Company or any other 3rd party for any Prohibited Use. During the Exclusivity Period, Licensor shall not license any Licensed Content to any Prohibited Company or any other 3rd party for any Prohibited Use. Notwithstanding the foregoing, Licensor may at any time license Immersive Imagery Data and Licensed Content for Government Applications, Internal Business Applications, and Private Domain Applications in accordance with the conditions indicated below. Licensor shall require that all licensees for Government Applications (i) restrict the licensee from providing Immersive Imagery Data or Licensed Content publicly for any use other than viewing, (ii) prohibit licensee from making the Immersive Imagery Data, or Licensed Content part of the public domain, or from allowing the Immersive Imagery Data or Licensed Content to become part of the public domain; (iii) prohibit licensee from allowing Immersive Imagery Data or Licensed Content to be downloaded. Licensor shall submit a report indicating to Google the format indicated in Exhibit A Section 6 in the event Licensor licenses imagery for more than [...] to the same Government Application licensee. If to Google, Licensor shall not be required to disclose the name of the Government Application licensee. In the event Licensor is prohibited from doing so. In the event Licensor licenses Immersive Imagery Data to a Private Domain licensee during the Blanket Exclusivity [...] Period, Licensor shall [...] for such [...] a ten (10) business day [...] such [...] Immersive [...]

Stefan Nowotny

Publicity and Secrecy

Variations on Intertwining Use

In the modern era, publicity is often depicted as the leading principle of political and social representation, in which there is no longer any room for secrecy. This is a myth, according to the Viennese philosopher

Stefan Nowontny. Publicity and secrecy are – through the production of affects – more entangled than ever in an inextricable knot.

One of the central myths of modernism is the narrative that the power of the secret has been replaced by publicity in this era. According to this narrative, the secret, previously a 'thoroughly acknowledged and necessary dimension of political agency',[1] was crucially discredited with the development of modernism.

Whereas the *secretarii* of the European princes and kings still administered a *secretum*, which derived its legitimacy from political power absolved from public concerns, it became the task of modern 'secretaries of state' to serve the public interest. And while the former were still agents of an instance of domination, which sought to present itself in the public eye, but was not responsible to the public in the modern sense, the modern approach was to prove the legitimacy of political agency specifically by carrying it out in a sphere of negotiation ideally accessible to all and actually co-determined by many.

This narrative can be regarded as a myth to the extent that it claims to provide information about the modern world from its origins – as it sometimes functions as part of what is a veritable cosmogony of modernism. Yet it is no less recognizable as a myth (or rather it is the coupling of these two moments that first justifies comprehending it as such) in that it can be understood as a kind of 'screen-narrative', which veils the origins it touches upon in the movement of its own revelation. It specifically represents those origins in a very particular way, the suggestive power of which can be explained also by the way it has established constant narrative elements, but still provides a place for all 'unsuitable' elements in a dark prehistory or somewhere else completely different. The expression 'screen-narrative' is clearly to be taken here as an allusion to Freud's concept of 'screen memories' (*Deckerinnerungen*): in emerging psychoanalytical theory, this referred to memories that 'represent' (and cover up at the same time) a whole complex of early experiences, of which large portions are subject to 'infantile amnesia', not least of all due to the effects of these kinds of superimposed representations, and which specifically cannot be recalled and made present. What is notable about these 'unrepresentable' memories here, is that despite their lack of realization, they sometimes lose nothing of their penetrating significance, so that they do not cease to exercise their recurrent influence.[2]

In this way, it is possible to consider that the narrative of publicity as a constitutive principle of the modern world overwrites a 'childhood', which has not been overcome by this world to the extent that the narrative claims, but which has instead simply become inaccessible to it, living on in it from this inaccessible place, all the more repressed in unpredictable turns and garbs. Let us consider the strange consequences of an assumption of this kind: it would mean that, rather than having overcome the secret, the power of publicity simply remains fraught with the power of the secret. Its most intrinsic secret is covered over in this way.

1. Lucian Hölscher, *Öffentlichkeit und Geheimnis. Eine begriffsgeschichtliche Untersuchung zur Entstehung der Öffentlichkeit in der frühen Neuzeit* (Stuttgart: Klett-Cotta, 1979), 7.

2. Cf. Sigmund Freud, 'Über Deckerinnerungen' [1899], in: idem, *Gesammelte Werke*, Vol. 1 (Frankfurt/M.: S. Fischer, 1964), 531–554; and the section 'Über die Deckerinnerungen', in: *Zur Psychopathologie des Alltagslebens* (Berlin: S. Karger, 1904), 15 ff.; in English, see the entry 'Screen Memory' in the *International Dictionary of Psychoanalysis*: http://www.enotes.com/psychoanalysis-encyclopedia/screen-memory.

And the task of an appropriate analysis would then be to trace the fates and reanimations of the secret in the midst of publicity, as well as that which publicity absolutely does not want to know of itself and therefore replaces with tendentious realizations.

Yet I do not want to take the analogy derived from psychoanalytical theory too far. What interests me here, first of all, is solely the position and the historical-epistemic configuration of a certain narrative, or more specifically: a certain *representation of publicity, which asserts publicity as the crucial principle of political and social representation and allows no more room within the organization of the modern world for the 'secret' – and yet without this world ever having left the secret behind.* In other words, I am interested in what Freud called, in reference to the covering power of certain realizations, the 'substitution in reproduction',[3] a substitution that specifically excludes 'other truly meaningful' elements of what there could be to realize from the capability of reproduction.

3. Freud, *Zur Psychopathologie des Alltagslebens*, op. cit. (note 3), 15.

Publicity, Secrecy, Modernity

On previous occasions, I have already discussed[4] several variations of these kinds of representations of public. One of them is to be found in Jürgen Habermas's depiction of the history of secret societies of the Enlightenment, the significance of which is that it was possible in them to 'practice the norms of political equality of a future

4. Cf. especially Stefan Nowotny, 'Clandestine Publics', trans. Aileen Derieg, in *transversal*, 03/2005, 'publicum': http://eipcp.net/transversal/0605/nowotny/en.

society'.[5] According to Habermas, in the milieu of absolutist authoritarian states in the eighteenth century, that circle still needed 'itself protection from becoming public . . . Its sphere of publicity still had to rely on secrecy', in order to be able to constitute itself at all on the basis of principles like freedom of discussion and egalitarian forms of exchange. As the bourgeois public sphere progressively prevailed, however, this circle saw itself confronted with an alternative: either to remain secret, but factiously falling 'prey to its own ideology', even inimical to the public, or to open up, to ensure 'relatively easy access', thus integrating into what they had basically always already anticipated, namely bourgeois society.[6] In short: where there was secrecy, sooner or later there had to be publicity – if one did not want to miss joining the modern world.

5. Jürgen Habermas, *Strukturwandel der Öffentlichkeit* (Frankfurt/M.: Suhrkamp, 1990), 14.

6. Ibid., 96.

During the period of the Enlightenment itself, there are equally unequivocal attempts to get rid of the dimension of secrecy. Here we encounter, so to speak, the work on its repression *in actu* – and at the same time the proposal of an *ideal* public, of which the characteristics could later be regarded as an actual principle of organization of bourgeois society. One relevant text in this context is the Appendix II of Kant's *Perpetual Peace*, where Kant argues that politics and morality can only be reconciled on the basis of the 'principle of publicity'. According to this principle, all maxims affecting the 'rights of other human beings' must be both *capable* of being made public and *in need* of being made public. The first demand, that they must be 'compatible with being made public',[7] is nothing other than a discrediting of the secret: for a maxim, which 'must at all costs be *kept secret*, if it is to succeed', can only be unjust, according to Kant, especially since the inevitable 'resistance of everyone', in the case of it becoming public, by itself may be the reason for secrecy. Kant places this first demand, which is ultimately a purely negative one because it aims at eliminating secrecy, alongside the demand for a requirement of publicity as the positive formulation of what he regards as the 'particular task of politics': to remain in harmony with the 'universal aim of the public (which is happiness)'.[8]

Politics is consequently to be conducted not only in public, but – as rational, moral, just politics – absolutely must harmonize with the public. It is noticeable, however, that the limitations of this kind of conception of political public already begin to emerge with Kant himself. This is the case where the same 'principle of publicity', which should actually ensure justice, obviously does the exact opposite and becomes a pillar of existing injustice. Kant touches on this kind of inversion of the moral-political function of publicity in the passages, in which he discusses the question of the lawfulness of overthrowing a tyrant[9] and describes the initial situation expressly: 'The rights of the people have been violated, and there can be no doubt that the tyrant would not be receiving unjust treatment if he were dethroned . . .' Yet as clear as this position is, the turn that follows it is all the more surprising. Despite the obvious injustice of the despotic rule, Kant sees every 'rebellion' against it as being in the wrong. This is specifically because a rebellion of this kind cannot fulfil the condition of 'making public' its maxims – unlike the sovereign, who may threaten with punishment of the 'ringleaders', for instance – without thwarting its own intentions: 'We are obliged to keep them [the maxims of rebellion] secret.'

Although no injustice is done to the unjust tyrant when he is dethroned, according to Kant's own statement, it is none other than the consistent application of the principle of publicity that leads to a condemnation of the concrete action that could result in the dethroning – and consequently to paradoxically siding with the ruler. The same formalism to which this taking sides is due, will subsequently move Kant to also declare every 'counter-insurrection' illegitimate, should a tyrant actually be dethroned. Nevertheless, the impression arises that the entire construction entrusting the reconciliation of politics and morality to the 'principle of publicity' rests on its own silent assumption, namely that injustice, which is to be eliminated with the help of publicity, is basically only a hypothetical injustice, not an actual one. As long as it has not yet been carried out, injustice may indeed be limited by the demand to make public the maxims on which it is based. In the case of an actual injustice, however, as the example of the tyrant shows, the relevant maxims no longer absolutely need to be kept secret, because it is specifically the inequalities stamped into publicity itself, which allow the despot, more than his adversaries, to publicly defend his regime of injustice.

7. Cf. Immanuel Kant, *Perpetual Peace* (1795) (Harmondsworth: Penguin Books, 2009), 58.

8. Cf. ibid., 65.

9. Cf. ibid., 60.

Hannah Arendt attempted to find a way out of the dead end that the Kantian argumentation led into in this respect, by pointing out a political categorical error on Kant's part: '. . . the alternative to established government is, for him [Kant], not revolution but a coup d'état. And a coup d'état, in contradistinction to a revolution, must indeed be prepared in secrecy, whereas revolutionary groups or parties have always been eager to make their goals public and to rally important sections of the population to their cause.'[10] This observation has the advantage of locating the nexus between publicity and power, mentioned by Kant only incidentally and one-sidedly, on the side of a revolutionary counter-power as well; in fact, it highlights an important difference in this nexus, namely that between a use of publicity that secures domination and one that empowers. Nevertheless, Arendt still remains true to the modern screen-narrative of the primacy of publicity over secrecy, of the repulsion of the latter by the former, as she identifies the – modern[11] – political option of revolution for her part solely with an agency oriented to the public sphere.

10. Hannah Arendt, *Lectures on Kant's Political Philosophy* (Chicago: University of Chicago Press, 1992), 60.

11. Cf. Hannah Arendt, *On Revolution* (Harmondsworth: Penguin Books, 1990), 12.

Super-Addressing and the Specter of Conspiration

These re-readings might be considered unusable and hardly up to date in a time when it has become conventional to conduct critical debates on publicity (at least in the 'West' or 'global North') in the midst of liberal democratic conditions, additionally oriented to the transformation that the organization of publicity has undergone and is undergoing due to new media and their forms of use. Are we seriously concerned today primarily with the question of overthrowing a tyrant? And are not the starting conditions today completely different, as a result of the increasingly densely interwoven possibilities of social networks, mobile communication and mobile audiovisual recording, than in the days of emerging press publicity and secret societies of the Enlightenment?

Certainly, these questions apply to principally important points. 'Public', as much as it may suggest the singular, is not to be considered as a uniform substance with constant essential properties, but rather always to be queried in terms of its institutional framework conditions and the technical, economic and social means of production that they engender. Nevertheless, idealized notions of the public as the sphere of a complete transparency, providing a kind of setting for negotiating political-social conflicts and thus for establishing just or at least less unjust conditions, seem to be deeply anchored in our political imaginary up to the present. If we do not wish to trust in the attempts to positively ground this idealization (for instance through its foundations in an expanded capacity of rationality), then publicity could be understood in this sense as a specifically modern ideological expression of a common 'super-addressee' of manifold articulation, or as Michail Bachtin says: as an instance simultaneously presupposed and staged by these articulations, which is supposed to vouch for an unclouded understanding and perfect responsivity.[12]

Moreover, the authoritarian 'tyrant' as the counterpart of these kinds of idealizations and ideologizations of publicity is still far from obsolete as well, specifically in the sense of a force that is based on secrecy, as well as in the sense of a force that has at its disposal an increased power of production and control in relation to articulations circulating in society. A more recent document for the construction of this kind of tyrannical counterpart is the Wikileaks Manifesto by Julian Assange from 2006, which provides little information about the positive reason for his own practice of publicizing, which has meanwhile attracted much attention, but instead portrays the opponents of this practice right at the beginning as 'authoritarian regimes', whose 'inner workings' are defined by 'conspiratorial interactions among the political elite'.[13] Here the conspiracy unmistakably designates the wolf in sheep's clothing, the tyrant in liberal democratic garb, which is further presented as the perfect correlate to the conspirative networks, of which it has itself the greatest horror: 'terrorist conspiracies'.

It is still attempted to banish the tyranny of the secret, yet still it returns, not infrequently as the spectre of conspiration. Experiences with the *real* history of 'publicity' have undoubtedly shown that much is hushed up or distorted in its name, and many are also hindered in their

12. Cf. Michail Bachtin, 'The problem of the text in linguistics, philology, and the human sciences: An experiment in philosophical analysis', in: *Speech genres & other late essays*, trans. Vern W. McGee, edited by Caryl Emerson and Michael Holquist (Austin: University of Texas Press, 1985), 126.

13. Cf. www.thecomment-factory.com/exclusive-the-wikileaks-manifesto-by-julian-assange-3342/ (accessed 1 July 2011); especially the section 'Authoritarian power is maintained by conspiracy'.

articulation. But the *ideal* of publicity is still upheld, and what falls short of this ideal is attributed to what this ideal has always sought to rid itself of: the secret. So attempts are undertaken to newly implement this ideal, whether by keeping – like the secret societies of the Enlightenment – one's own operations to this end secret, or by forming 'anonymous' networks to support these operations. Regardless of how the concrete actions of Wikileaks are judged, the result is an impulse for reflection on the relationship between publicity and secret that was already formulated by Negt and Kluge: 'Alternating between an idealizing and a critical view of the public sphere leads ... only to an ambivalent result: the public sphere sometimes appears as something that can be used, another time as something that cannot be used.'[14]

14. Oskar Negt and Alexander Kluge, *Öffentlichkeit und Erfahrung. Zur Organisationsanalyse von bürgerlicher und proletarischer Öffentlichkeit* (Frankfurt/M.: Suhrkamp, 1972), 20.

Can the Revolution Be Internetized?

Against this background, let us consider in more detail an episode that occurred, far less spectacularly, shortly after the Wikileaks publications at the end of the last year – specifically in the course of events that actually overthrew a tyrant (even if not necessarily the power structures that supported him). On 27 January 2011, bilingual (Arabic/English) excerpts from a '26-page pamphlet' were published in the Internet edition of *The Atlantic*, which had been circulated among Egyptian rebels. Under the heading 'Egyptian Activists' Action Plan: Translated',[15]

15. Cf. for the following quotations: www.theatlantic.com/international/archive/2011/01/egyptian-activists-action-plan-translated/70388/.

it was announced with a certain pride: 'Egyptian activists have been circulating a kind of primer to Friday's planned protest. We were sent the plan by two separate sources and have decided to publish excerpts here, with translations into English. Over Twitter, we connected with a translator, who translated the document with exceptional speed.'

One might perhaps conjecture that this involved the 'Arendtian' case of a revolution 'eager to make its goals public and to rally important sections of the population to its cause'. And in fact, on the second page of the material published by *The Atlantic*, the goals are expressly named, under the heading 'The Demands of the Egyptian People', of what was already clearly recognizable as the attempt of a revolution: from overthrowing the Mubarak regime through general formulas like freedom and justice, all the way to the constructive tasks of forming a new government devoted to the interests of the Egyptians and setting up a corresponding administration. But a single page was sufficient for this. As soon as it was a matter of the question of *how* further sections of the population were to be included, the relevant calls – 'shout slogans in the name of Egypt and the people's freedom', 'positive slogans', 'positive language', etc. – were embedded in *tactical* instructions, such as 'assemble with your friends and neighbors in residential streets far away from where the security forces are', or 'go out into the major streets in very large groups in order to form the biggest possible assembly'. The maxims that were circulated here were obviously not exhausted in publicizing the *goals* of action, but rather related more to a *prudence* of action, which was closely connected to the goals (a coup d'état ultimately does not necessarily need to include large sections of the population), but by no means equated with them. And this prudence includes, not least of all, the attempt of a differentiated way of dealing with publics and distribution media – which *The Atlantic* also did not fail to mention: 'As you'll read, the creators of the pamphlet explicitly asked that the pamphlet not be distributed on Twitter or Facebook, only through email or other contacts. We're publishing this piece of ephemera because we think it's a fascinating part of the historical record of what may end up becoming a very historic day for Egypt.'

The only problem was that by publishing the material on their own website, *The Atlantic* obviously torpedoed the prudence of 'the creators', probably because, as the last sentence suggests, it was not possible to resist the temptation to document a history that had not yet really occurred. Obsessed with publishing, those responsible thus revealed a glaring illiteracy in relation to the differential *handling* of publicity structures and circulation media. As was to be expected, the protests very quickly followed – which is evident on the one hand in the posts published on the website, but on the other also in the following editorial 'Update', which appeared online only 41 minutes after the publication of the material: 'People have asked why these particular pages were chosen. We had limited resources, so we knew we'd only be able to translate an excerpt. My guiding principles were to stay away from the small amount of tactical information in the pamphlet. Instead, we ran the more general pages. There is nothing in these pages that goes beyond standard advice and broad political statements.'

'Stay away from the small amount of tactical information'? The 'more general pages' that were published still included guidelines for choosing demonstration routes, on questions of clothing and sign codes or even on accessories such as spray cans or pot lids (which were recommended for use as protective shields). The pamphlet was headed with the title 'How to protest intelligently', which quite unambiguously indicated its primarily tactical character, and the adjective 'intelligently' could mentally be added to the heading on the last page as well, specifically 'How to publish and disseminate this information'. This last page also included the sentence: 'Do not betray your fellow citizens and ensure that this not fall into the hands of anyone who works for the police.'

There is no need to speculate about whether the Egyptian security forces really needed *The Atlantic* to obtain this kind of material. It is certain, however, that *The Atlantic* made their job easier rather than harder, and that this was due to an astonishingly unintelligent reissue of the aforementioned imperative that where even just remainders of secrecy are to be found, they must be made public as quickly as possible.

'What I Can Share with You Is Deeply Troubling'

Among the sometimes bizarre, but no less consequential reprises of the modern dramas involving publicity, the case of the infamous speech held by Colin Powell on 5 February 2003 before the United Nations Security Council is especially interesting. The point of this speech was to convince the 'international public' – both in the sense of an institutional representation in the form of UN bodies, and in the sense of 'public opinion' (as a social circulation phenomenon far more difficult to grasp) – of the existence of weapons of mass destruction in Iraq and the unavoidableness of the war that had been long prepared. Here 'facts' were presented, based on intelligence material from various 'sources', intended to support the legality of a maxim, of which it could certainly be said that it relates to 'the rights of other people' (Kant). The precise character of these 'sources' was of course – especially since they were from secret services – only very vaguely revealed; it was consequently hardly possible to check these 'facts', which were expressly only incompletely presented: 'The material I will present to you comes from a variety of sources. Some are U.S. sources. And some are those of other countries. . . . I cannot tell you everything that we know. But what I can share with you, when combined with what all of us have learned over the years, is deeply troubling. . . . My colleagues, every statement I make today is backed up by sources, solid sources. These are not assertions. What we're giving you are facts and conclusions based on solid intelligence. I will cite some examples, and these are from human sources. . . . Ladies and gentlemen, these are not assertions. These are facts, corroborated by many sources, some of them sources of the intelligence services of other countries.'[16]

16. Cf. 'Full text of Colin Powell's speech. US secretary of state's address to the United Nations security council', www.guardian.co.uk/world/2003/feb/05/iraq.usa (accessed 1 July 2011).

Whereas Colin Powell's appearance before the United Nations thus seems to uphold the demand for publicity in relation to one's own maxim, the actual justification for this maxim remained entrusted to an area, of which the lack of publication capability did not even appear to be worth mentioning. For as a 'thoroughly recognized and necessary dimension of political action', the secret still applies, despite all publicity imperatives, at least where it involves the dimension of intelligence gathered by secret services. In other words, Powell's speech was not really intended to make the maxim for action of the Bush administration public for discussion. Instead, it was more a matter of (re-)performing the modern ritual of publicity as credibly as possible – but at the same time shifting the aspects of this ritual that have to do with legitimation disputes from the maxim for action itself into a 'secret' area again that remains elusive to them.

In the case of Powell's speech, this shift was drowned out by the mantra of 'sources', 'facts', even 'conclusions'. It is as though these required no discussion, but were instead solidified simply through the tautological insistence that they actually existed. The three-part mantra roughly followed a certain pattern: (1) the facts are facts, not assertions; (2) they are facts because they are based on sources, which are real sources, even if they are not documented; and (3) the conclusions that we draw from them are, because of (1) and (2), real and unassailable conclusions.

Naturally this kind of 'argumentation' can hardly hold up to critical epistemological requirements, and we have long known that it was simply false. Yet a capability for critique was never the point of this publicity spectacle, but rather it was to forestall every possible critique by withdrawing everything it could be founded upon into a 'secret' area. A suggestive audiovisual presentation spectacle took the place of a negotiable issue, and at the same time an incidental revelation of the – here also tactically defined – boundary between public and secret: 'What I can share with you . . . is deeply troubling.' One could also add: And *how* I will share it with you will give you the *feeling* that it is deeply troubling, because that is, first and foremost, what you have to know.

The use value of publicity – or rather the specific intertwining of the use of publicity and secret – shows itself here closely linked with the production of affect-political effects, which result from techniques of valorising or devaluing signs. And perhaps it is exactly in this that we find a crucial indication of how the question of the relation of publicity and secret should be posed today: as a question about the production of affects (certainties, anxieties, insecurities, feelings of solidarity, resentments, etcetera) through signs that are established on the unstable boundary between publicity and secret. For what the modern myth of publicity covers up is, among others, the circumstance that power (whether securing domination or even emancipatory) is developed by whoever controls the boundary between publicity and secret, indeed by whoever continually reinvents it.

Translator's note: on the use of the term 'publicity', cf. Stefan Nowotny, 'The Condition of Becoming Public', in *transversal*, 09 2003, http://www.eipcp.net/transversal/1203/nowotny/en: 'As familiar as the term "public" may seem to us as a central category of political modernism, reaching a precise understanding of it raises a number of difficulties. These difficulties already become apparent in the question of the translation of the German word "Öffentlichkeit", the characteristic political-social meaning of which was established in the late 18th century as a translation of the French "publicité": In English (and the case is similar for French), the German "Öffentlichkeit" is translated in certain contexts as "public" or "publicity"; however, where "Öffentlichkeit" stands for a general category of social organization, "public sphere" or "public space" is usually preferred. While this indicates a certain ambiguity in the German term, it also expresses a problem: translating "Öffentlichkeit" as "public sphere" causes a level of meaning to vanish that is nonetheless central to the modern idea of the public - specifically that "Öffentlichkeit" not only refers to a *category* in political modernism, but most of all a *principle* of social organization. This means that it is not simply a given "sphere" (or plurality of spheres) – regardless of how it is organized – of modern societies, but rather a central *mode* of their organization and constitution. . . . It should be noted that this is not solely a matter of reconstructing the meaning of "publicity" as a principle of social organization, but rather also of calling attention to the conditions of a certain disappearance of this meaning of "publicity". This disappearance is also symptomatically evident in that the English word "publicity" (like the French "publicité"), to which the meaning of a principle of social organization is certainly attributed in contexts of political theory, has been largely overlaid in everyday language with meanings that refer to the areas of advertising, marketing or media attention industries.

Boris Groys

WikiLeaks

The Revolt of the Clerks, or Universality as Conspiracy

Media theorist Boris Groys analyses the significance of WikiLeaks against the background of the democratic need for universal openness and communication. In doing so, he makes a remark-able observation: WikiLeaks' universal openness is based on total concealment, and this makes it a first example of a truly postmodern universal conspiracy. By devoting itself to being a universal, administrative service in the form of a conspiracy, WikiLeaks is not only a historic innovation – it also runs a great risk.

We have become accustomed to protests and revolts in the name of particular identities and interests – revolts in the name of universal projects, such as liberalism or communism, seem to belong to the past. But the activities of WikiLeaks serve no specific identities or interests. They rather have a general, universal goal: to guarantee the free flow of information. Thus, the phenomenon of WikiLeaks signals a return of universalism into politics. This fact alone makes the emergence of WikiLeaks highly significant. We know from history that only universalist projects can lead to real political change. WikiLeaks signals not only a return of universalism but also the deep transformation that the notion of universalism has undergone during recent decades. WikiLeaks is not a political party. It does not offer any universalist vision of society, political programme, or ideology designed to 'spiritually' or politically unify mankind. Rather, WikiLeaks offers a sum of technical means that allows universal access to any specific, particular content. The universality of idea is here substituted by the universality of access. WikiLeaks offers not a universalist political project but a universal information service. The ethos of WikiLeaks is the ethos of civil, administrative service – globalized and universalized.

In his famous essay 'La trahison des clercs' (1927) Julien Benda aptly described this ethos – and a new universal class defined by it. He called its members 'clerks'. The word 'clerk' is often translated as 'intellectual'. But,

in fact, the intellectual is for Benda precisely a protagonist of the betrayal of the clerk's ethos, because the intellectual prefers the universality of his or her ideas to the duty of universal service. The true clerk does not commit himself to any particular worldview – even the most universalist one. The clerk, rather, serves others by helping them to realize their own particular ideas and goals. Benda saw the clerk primarily as a functionary, as an administrator in the framework of the enlightened, democratic state that is ruled by law. However, today the concept of the state has lost the aura of universality that it still had when Benda wrote his book. The state – even if it is internally organized in the most universalist way – remains a national state. Its clerks, notwithstanding their universalist ethos, are necessarily embedded in the apparatuses of power that pursue particular, national interests. This embedment is one of the reasons why the traditional clerk ethos, as it was described by Benda, became somewhat suspect.

However, I would argue that today we are witnessing a rebirth of the clerk – and of the clerk ethos. Internet clerks have replaced state clerks. The Internet was hailed originally as a chance to transcend and undermine the power of state bureaucracy. From the contemporary perspective it becomes obvious though that the Internet simply transferred the ethos and functions of the universal class from the state clerks to the Internet clerks. However, this transition did not go smoothly. And WikiLeaks is the best example of problems with which the new universalism is confronted in our contemporary world.

This new universalism sees its main political and cultural task in achieving the universal representation of multiple and heterogeneous cultural perspectives that are dictated by different cultural identities, gender and class determinations and personal histories of their subjects. One tries not to exclude any of these perspectives from what one can call universal exposure. This seems to lead to a certain downgrading of the universal because it signals a lack of faith in a possibility of universalist projects or ideas that would be open to all of mankind – and could unify it. Seemingly, the new Internet universalism leaves mankind spiritually, ideologically, culturally and politically divided – even if it becomes informationally and technically united. But things are not so simple. The historically known universalist projects were born out of the traditional religious and philosophical desire to transcend one's own particular perspective and reach a universal perspective that is open and relevant for everybody. It is the deep distrust towards the possibility of such an act of transcendence that discredited universalism during the twentieth century. However, the possibility remains open to reject one's own particular perspective without transcending it, without opening any universalist perspective. The act of transcendence is substituted here by an act of radical reduction. This reduction produces a subjectivity

without an identity – or, rather, with zero-identity.

We tend to understand subjectivity as a bearer of a certain individual, original message, as a source of a unified worldview, as a producer of specific, personal, individual meanings. But there is a possibility of a subjectivity without an individual message or worldview – a neutral, anonymous subjectivity producing no original, individual meanings or opinions at all. In fact, such a subjectivity is not simply a theoretical possibility but an ever more present reality nowadays. It is a subjectivity of the subjects that do not want to express their own ideas, or insights, or desires – but merely to create possibilities, the conditions for other subjectivities to express their ideas, opinions, worldviews and desires. I would call these subjects universal subjects. They are not universal subjects because they transcend their particular viewpoints towards a universal viewpoint. Rather, they simply erase everything private, personal and particular through a peculiar act of self-reduction. They are neutral, anonymous subjects – not the meta-subjects of classical theology or metaphysics but, so to say, infra-subjects – populating the infrastructure of contemporary life.

They are clerks in Benda's sense of the word, creating the universal infrastructural, networking, rhisomatic conditions that allow other people to satisfy their particular desires and realize their particular projects. The infrastructure of the Internet is today the privileged place for the current generation of clerks. They run companies like Microsoft, Google, Facebook, Wikipedia, etcetera. And WikiLeaks belongs, in fact, in the same mould, because it does not seek to relay its own message, but only to transport the messages of others – even if it does mean to distribute these messages ever further against the will of their producers. The subjectivity of the clerk cannot be deconstructed because it does not construct any meanings. It is in itself a medium – and not the message. It immunizes itself against any opinions and meanings that it perceives as signs of corruption. The clerks are all-inclusive because they are all-exclusive. They have pure service mentality and ethics. They may have their secrets – but these secrets just wait to be revealed as new means of communication that will again be open for everybody. They build, indeed, something like a contemporary universal class that does not have any own ideas and goals – even universal ideas and goals. Instead of expressing his or her own views the clerk creates the conditions for others to express their views. This operation is in no way innocent, however.

Let us assume that the strategy of inclusion of every existing worldview and cultural perspective into the global media networks of universal exposure has been successful. And there are some indications that it can be successful in the long run: the Internet and other contemporary means of communication offer – at least potentially – the possibility to avoid censorship and exclusion and to make everyone's particular message universally accessible. However, we are all well aware today of the fate of any subjective message, particular viewpoint or individual idea – the fate to which they are necessarily submitted after they are put into circulation through the media of communication. We have heard already from Marshall McLuhan that the message of the medium undermines, subverts and shifts every individual message using this medium. We heard from Heidegger that *die Sprache spricht* (the language speaks), and not so much the individual that is using the language. These formulations undermine the subjectivity of the speaker, of the sender of the message – even if the hermeneutical subjectivity of the listener, reader or receiver of the information seems to be left relatively intact. However, Derridian deconstruction and Deleuzian machines of desire also got rid of this last avatar of subjectivity. Here, an individual reading of a text or interpretation of an image goes down in the infinite sea of interpretations and/or is carried away by the impersonal flows of desire. Mastery over communication is revealed by contemporary media theory as a subjective illusion. This incapacity of the subject to formulate, stabilize and communicate its message through the media is often characterized as the 'death of the subject'.

Thus, we are confronted with a somewhat paradoxical situation. On the one hand, in our epoch we believe in the necessity of inclusion of all subjects with all their particular messages into the networks of universal exposure and communication. On the other, howeve, we know that we are unable to guarantee unity and stability of these messages after this act of inclusion. The information flows dissolve, shift and subvert all the individual messages by turning them into more or less accidental aggregates of floating signifiers. Believing in the politics of inclusion, we no less strongly believe in the unavoidable death of the included subjects – together with their particular messages – through the same act of inclusion. Looking at the Internet as the leading medium of our time we find ourselves confronted with a potentially anonymous mass of texts and images in which their particular origins – together with the particular intentions of their authors – have been erased. The copy-and-paste operation that defines the functioning of the digital media turns any individual expression into an anonymous, impersonal readymade that can be used by any Internet user at any moment. The universal presents itself through the Internet as an impersonal sign flow. The subjectivities of the 'content providers' unavoidably drown in this flow. In this sense the new universality – universality of Internet clerks – creates a universal image after all. It is not a universal idea, project or commitment but, rather, a universal event – a fact that the sign flow took this and not that form at a particular moment in time.

Julian Assange eloquently describes this new, if one will, postmodern, post-historical universalist vision in a recent interview with Hans-Ulrich Obrist (in: e-flux/journal, no. 24, 25): 'There's a universe of information, and we can imagine a sort of Platonic ideal in which we have an infinite horizon of information. It's similar to the concept of the Tower of Babel. Imagine a field before us composed of all the information that exists in the world – inside government computers, people's letters, things that have already been published, the stream of information coming out of televisions, this total knowledge of all the world, both accessible and inaccessible to the public. We can as a thought experiment observe this field and ask: If we want to use information to produce actions that affect the world to make it more just, which information will do that?'

This vision is especially striking by how un-Platonic and even anti-Platonic it is. Plato hoped to find his 'Platonic' ideas beyond the stream of information. And Plato tried to find these ideas in people's thinking – not in what they have written or archived. He looked for something stable, permanent, being able to withstand the flow of impressions and thoughts – and at the same time immediately evident, radiant, beautiful. Now Assange also assumes that the information that does not move, that remains stable, is the most interesting. But his reasons to think so are equally very un-Platonic. In the same interview he says: 'Some of the information in this tremendous field, if you look at it carefully, is faintly glowing. And what it's glowing with is the amount of work

that's being put into suppressing it . . .
So, if you search for that signal of suppression, then you can find all this information that you should mark as information that should be released. So, it was an epiphany to see the signal of censorship to always be an opportunity, to see that when organizations or governments of various kinds attempt to contain knowledge and suppress it, they are giving you the most important information you need to know: that there is something worth looking at to see if it should be exposed and that censorship expresses weakness, not strength.' In other words: the epiphany here is not a Platonic epiphany, not an ecstasy of evidence. It is, rather, a negative epiphany leading to a moral obligation to liberate information from captivity and to let it flow. The concept of the information flow is here obviously the normative, regulatory, universal idea – even if it is a very un-Platonic one. At the same time, the criterion of universality obviously remains an aesthetic as well as an ethical one. The censorship, the artificial interruption of the sign flow is perceived here as an attempt to distort the sublime vision of the universal landscape of knowledge. Particular interests tried to damage this vision, even though they had already been recognized as irrelevant and obsolete.

And, indeed, the particular subjectivities that were already theoretically deconstructed and practically expropriated through the Internet become here reconstructed artificially as owners of a 'private sphere' – an area of private access that is supposed to remain secret. In our media-driven, postdeconstructive age the dead subject has become a secret. The individual is defined today by the pass codes and passwords that delineate his or her area of access. The area of access is assumed at the same time to be protected and concealed. Thus the area of access substitutes the unity of the individual message, the personal, authorial intention, the subjective act of thinking and feeling. Technical protection replaces metaphysical certainty. For a very long time subjectivity was understood as being metaphysically inaccessible – as something that can be only interpreted but not directly experienced. Today we no longer believe in this metaphysical place of subjectivity. Thus, hermeneutics have been replaced by hacking. The hacker overcomes the borders of individual subjectivity that is understood as an area of privileged access. It opens its secret and appropriates its message – instead of interpreting it. And he releases this message – and lets the media networks dissolve it.

In this sense the activity of WikiLeaks is a practical continuation of Derridian deconstruction. It is a practice that liberates the signs that are captured and controlled by subjectivity. The difference is only this: in the case of Internet we have to do not with the metaphysical but with purely technical control over the signs. Accordingly, hacking is used here instead of philosophical critique. Hacking is often criticized as an intrusion into the private sphere but, in fact, the *telos* of all contemporary media is the complete abolition of the private sphere. Traditional media do nothing but hunt down celebrities to reveal their personal lives. In a certain sense WikiLeaks does the same in the framework of the Internet. Not accidentally, it cooperates with the international press – *The New York Times*, *Der Spiegel*, etcetera. The abolishment and confiscation of the private sphere (but not of private property!) is what unites WikiLeaks with traditional media. Wikileaks can be seen as an avant-garde of the media. But it is not a rebellion against it. Rather, Wikileaks moves more audaciously and faster in the direction of the common *telos* of the modern and contemporary media by realizing the goal of the universal class – new universalization of the world through the means of universal service.

But here a following question arises: In what respect and to what degree is this universal service inscribed into the contemporary market economy, into the contemporary global flow of capital that also pretends to be a neutral, non-ideological and universally accessible means for achieving private goals and satisfying private desires? It is obvious that the corporations operating the different aspects of the Internet are totally inscribed into the global capitalist markets. But what about WikiLeaks? Its attacks are directed more against state censorship than against the flow of capital. One can formulate the fol-lowing hypothesis concerning the atti-tude of WikiLeaks towards capitalism. From the perspective of WikiLeaks capital is not universal enough, because it is ultimately dependent on the patronage of the national states and relies on their political, military and industrial power. That is why mainstream Internet corporations col-laborate with state censorship and block the free flow of information through different means of protection. As a rule, we think about capitalism as a power that corrupts the state – the democratic, universalist, national state. But WikiLeaks indirectly reverses this accusation. And, indeed, one can see the situation from another perspective: capitalism does not fulfil its global promise because it is perma-nently corrupted by the national states and their security interests. In this perspective, WikiLeaks offers a per-spective of a universal service that exceeds the universality of capitalism – that is more radically global than the global markets.

The practice of WikiLeaks is often discussed and criticized in terms of invasion and breach of privacy. But, in fact, this practice does not affect the privacy of private individuals so much. For sure, Assange, as many others from the Internet crowd, does not believe in copyrights and, in general, the rights of individuals to block the flow of information. But his activity is mostly directed against so-called state privacy – because state censorship seems to contradict the promise of universality that was and is still given by the modern state. In this sense the breach of state privacy simply means the restoration of the original goal of the state, giving the state a chance to move towards a greater universality.

Thus one can say that WikiLeaks is an expression of the revolt of the clerks against the betrayal of their ethos, of their universal vocation by the national states. And the cause of this betrayal is seen by Wikileaks in the incapability of the existing state apparatuses to become truly universal by redefining their national interests in a universal perspective. But now the question arises: Is radical, uncompromising universality possible at all? The answer is yes – but under one condition: the universal has to become isolated, protected from the world of particularities that is constantly corrupting it.

And, indeed, to remain truly universalist any universal project should be protected from corruption, for instance from the private, particular interests that could undermine its universality. But if a universal project has been designed as open and publicly accessible it necessarily becomes corrupted because the realization of this project unavoidably involves compromises with exiting institutions and private interests. The only way to avoid corruption and to keep the universality of a universal project and its realization intact is to separate this project from the outside world as radically as possible – to make this project publicly inaccessible. Or, in other words, the universality can function in our world of particularities only in a form of conspiracy and only under the conditions of perfect inaccessibility, non-transparency and obscurity. Otherwise, it will be immediately betrayed and corrupted.

The conspiratorial dimension of universality is historically well known. The politics of conspiracy is characteristic of all religious sects and revolutionary groups having a universal claim. And this conspiratorial politics was time and again criticized in the name of openness, democracy and universal public access. The critique saw the reason for their rigorous politics of conspiracy and exclusion, primarily, in the narrow and exclusive character of the ideologies that the individual religious sects or revolutionary groups have professed. Or, in other words, the critique saw this reason in their commitment to the notion of universal truth. Every truth that was professed by these sects and groups raised a claim to be universal – but at the same time it remained particular because it was defined from the beginning in an opposition to other truths raising the same universal claim. This paradox of universal truth was made responsible for ideologically motivated conspiracies and politics of exclusion. Accordingly, the remedy was seen in the rejection of the notion of universal truth as such. The universal truth was substituted by a plurality of identities and perspectives that was supposed to not lead to any radical conflict – because all of these identities and perspectives lacked the universal claim that could provoke a real conflict between them. It is the political reason behind the substitution of the universal idea, or universal truth by universal access and universal service.

But now the practice of WikiLeaks demonstrates that universal access can be also provided only in the form of universal conspiracy. In the same interview mentioned before, Assange says: 'It was not just the intellectual challenge of making and breaking these cryptographic codes and connecting people together in novel ways. Rather, our will came from a quite extraordinary notion of power, which was that with some clever mathematics you can, very simply – and this seems complex in abstraction but simple in terms of what computers are capable of – enable any individual to say no to the most powerful state. So if you and I agree on a particular encryption code, and it is mathematically strong, then the forces of every superpower brought to bear on that code still cannot crack it. So a state can desire to do something to an individual, yet it is simply not possible for the state to do it – and in this sense, mathematics and individuals are stronger than superpowers.' And later Assange described a possibility of a name for an URL that can protect its content far beyond any possibility of its protection by the conventional copyright regulations.

In other words, universal public access is possible only under the conditions of a complete inaccessibility of the means that guarantee this accessibility. Transparency is based on radical non-transparency. Universal openness is based on the most perfect

closure. WikiLeaks is a first example of a truly postmodern universal conspiracy. It operates beyond any claim to truth – universal or particular. But at the same time it demonstrates that universal access is possible only as universal conspiracy. Not accidentally, Assange refers time and again in his texts and interviews to Solzhenitsyn as the main source of his inspiration. And, indeed, the whole activity of Solzhenitsyn can be described as a clever combination of conspiracy and publicity. As many other Soviet dissidents of that time he discovered the international press as a source of power that is comparable with the power of the Soviet State. And as the other Soviet dissidents – at least during his Soviet time – he did not profess any ideology. He simply wanted to give testimony. He wanted to provide access to what was hidden. But to be able do so, he, as well as other dissidents, had to be highly conspiratorial.

Now the trajectory of WikiLeaks becomes understandable: it interprets and embodies the universal service as conspiracy – and conspiracy as universal service. And this understanding puts WikiLeaks itself and its members at risk. Already in the 1930s Alexandre Kojève proclaimed in his famous lectures on Hegel that the history of the universal visions is over, that the human being has ceased to be a subject of truth and became a sophisticated animal having only particular interests and desires. For Kojève that meant that the posthistorical mode of existence excludes the possibility of substantial risk because such a possibility arises only as a result of commitment of the subject to a universal truth. Thus, for Kojève the only possibility to remain a philosopher after the end of history was to enter the universal service in a form of European administration. And Kojève understood the way of universal service and administration as a secure one. Now WikiLeaks and Assange himself proved that the way of universal service can also lead to a substantial risk. They became dissidents of universal service – and invented in this way a new form of risk. Or, rather, they thematized this risk and made it explicit by committing themselves to universal service and administration in a form of conspiracy from the very beginning. It is a true historical innovation. And it is to be expected that this innovation will have interesting consequences.

Jodi Dean

Know It All

WikiLeaks, Democracy and the Information Age

According to American political theorist Jodi Dean, WikiLeaks' Julian Assange lacks insight into the setting in which he operates. In communicative capitalism, the whole concept of the relation between openness and democracy radically changed. Not only does Assange assume that reliable, symbolically effective information is the basis of democracy, he also does not recognize that information overkill is a greater handicap than too little information, and that he himself is part of the spectacle that is diverting attention from political issues.

Introducing her extensively mediated (live audience of 1,800 people, live web stream, Facebook and Twitter updates, radio broadcast, print coverage) two-hour long conversation with Julian Assange and Slavoj Žižek, Amy Goodman, host of the US radio program, 'Democracy Now!', asserted that 'information is power' and 'information is a matter of life and death'.[1]

She illustrated her point by linking two instances of a US Apache helicopter in Iraq firing on seemingly innocent people. The first occurred in February 2007 when a helicopter with the call sign 'Crazy Horse' fired on men raising their arms in surrender. An account of the incident appeared among the 400,000 documents released by WikiLeaks as the Iraq War Logs late in the summer of 2010. The second event took placed in July 2007 when a helicopter with the same call sign fired on an unarmed group, killing two journalists and wounding some children. WikiLeaks released video shots from the helicopter gun-sight under the title 'Collateral Murder' in April 2010.[2]

Goodman concluded: 'Now, I dare say that if we had seen what came out in the Iraq War Logs in February of 2007, if we had learned the story at the time, after it happened, of the men with their hands up trying to surrender, there would have been an outcry. People are good. People care. People are compassionate. They would have called for an investigation. Perhaps one would have begun. But it might well have saved the lives of so many. Certainly, months later, perhaps that same Apache helicopter unit under investigation would not have done what it did. And maybe Namir Noor-Eldeen, the young Reuters videographer, and his driver Saeed Chmagh, not to mention the other men who were killed and the kids critically injured, none of that would have happened to them. That's why information matters. It is important we know what is done in our name. And today we're going to talk about this new age of information.'

For Goodman, information is so powerful that its very presence generates consensus, conviction and action without doubt or ambiguity. Despite the deep divisions in the USA and throughout the world with respect to US militarism, the war in Iraq and the so-called war on terror, and regardless of the way these divisions manifest themselves in multiple media outlets, and notwithstanding US Americans' overall deep mistrust of media, information about the first event is ostensibly so clear and unambiguous that it could 'certainly' save lives (well, 'maybe', 'perhaps'). This is a strange claim for our contemporary setting. Images of torture and official acknowledgment of torture have not resulted in any serious investigations, trials, reprimands or sentencing of key officials. The leaked videos themselves were met with questioning and disagree-

1. 'Exclusive: Julian Assange of WikiLeaks & Philosopher Slavoj Žižek in Conversation with Amy Goodman' (5 July 2011). Available at http://www.democracynow.org/2011/7/5/exclusive_julian_assange_of_WikiLeaks_philosopher. Unless otherwise noted, this is the source for all subsequent references.

2. Available at http://www.collateralmurder.com/en/index.html.

ment. Ultimately, they were displaced from view by more intense focus on the one man behind their release and circulation, Assange.

At least three suppositions underlie Goodman's conviction. The first is that information is immediate and efficient. Information can be transmitted from one location to another with no decay of meaning, no noise, no distortion. The second supposition is that of an underlying trust. Those who receive the information believe it and understand its significance. They are not sceptical, cynical or malevolent – *people are good, people are compassionate, people care*. The third is that the relation between knowledge and action is obvious and direct. In Socratic terms, 'to know the good is to do the good'. Information is the knowledge necessary for action, the missing link between acquiescence and resistance, passive acceptance and active work to change the world. The basic matrix for Goodman's conviction, then, is democratic. She assumes that secrets withheld from the people are barriers to their exercise of political power. And, conversely, the secrets people (whether as individuals, corporations or shadowy associations of hackers) withhold from governments likewise constitute barriers to state power. Secrets contain the information needed to act. It thus bears emphasizing that the democratic matrix is also the matrix of conspiracy theory. Insofar as the secret is the locus of a missing legitimacy, a hidden crime or corruption that, once revealed, can be weeded out and rightful authority

restored, the conspiracy theorist pursues the same endeavour as the democrat. Both are suspicious of what they see and want to get to the real truth – one of the reasons that Jeremy Bentham defended publicity as a system of distrust.[3]

3. For a detailed account of secrecy, conspiracy and democracy, see Jodi Dean, *Publicity's Secret* (Ithaca, NY: Cornell University Press, 2002).

Goodman's suppositions do not hold under communicative capitalism. Despite her gesture to 'this new age of information', Goodman doesn't acknowledge what is new about this age, that is, what abundant contributions to a rapidly circulating flow of intensities entail for the effectiveness of any particular contribution.[4] Communicative capitalism is characterized by the decline of symbolic efficiency. As theorized by Slavoj Žižek, the decline of symbolic efficiency points to the failure of symbols and messages to produce expected responses, that is, to a fundamental uncertainty regarding what they mean or whether they are reliable.[5] There are always other possibilities. What is obvious to some is unclear or suspicious to others. Indeed, there is no stopping point at which to resolve the uncertainties; reflexivity goes all the way down. The very conditions of possibility for adequation are missing. Images and affects rush in to fill the gap – does someone appear trustworthy? How did she seem? Did she seem believable or was something a little

4. For a more detailed account of communicative capitalism, see Jodi Dean, *Democracy and Other Neoliberal Fantasies* (Durham, NC: Duke University Press, 2009).

5. Slavoj Žižek, *The Ticklish Subject* (Londen: Verso, 1999), p. 326.

off? The ability to falsify is unlimited. The lack of a capacity to know is the other side of the abundance of knowledge. It's no surprise, then, that the decline of symbolic efficiency is accompanied by a decline in a sense of the capacity for action. Because we can never be certain, we always need more information. The implication of the decline of symbolic efficiency is thus that secrets don't contain the information needed to act. They are just tags like any other, except with a bit more intensity attached – we want to know, but after we do, we move on to something else.

The administration of George W. Bush was well-adapted to the media environment of communicative capitalism. To deal with the home front of the Iraq war, it groomed former generals into talking heads. Not only did these 'military analysts' advocate war and parrot administration talking points, many were also tied to the defence industry as executives, consultants and board members. According to *The New York Times*: 'Internal Pentagon documents repeatedly refer to the military analysts as "message force multipliers" or "surrogates" who could be counted on to deliver administration "themes and messages" to millions of Americans "in the form of their own opinions".'[6]

6. David Barstow, 'Behind TV Analysts, Pentagon's Hidden Hand', *The New York Times* (20 April 2008). Available at http://www.nytimes.com/2008/04/20/us/20generals.html?pagewanted=all.

The term 'message force multipliers' can be accented in at least two ways: the force multiplication of messages or the multiplication of message forces.[7] Force multiplication indexes a communications strategy for a complex media environment. It implies adding lots of forces, putting more people on the ground or on the air, just as one would send more troops into a situation. 'Multiplication of message forces' indicates a concrete awareness of the affective dimension of media in communicative capitalism. The Bush administration excelled in excepting itself from the signifying aspect of language and relying instead on affective prompts. It absorbed the lesson from advertising and pop music: repetition exerts a force, a compulsion; repetition has effects independent of the meaning of what is repeated. Repetition itself has an affective impact – a sexualizing pulsation, a threatening intrusion, a hilarious extreme. State politics in the twenty-first century in the USA, UK and Europe has become ever more adept at tying together previously stable meanings in ways that rely on and at the same time disrupt these meanings. This combination of reliance and disruption generates affective responses from the tension accompanying the combustion of meaning and non-meaning.

7. The following discussion summarizes an argument I develop in more detail in *Blog Theory* (Cambridge, UK: 2010).

The combination also suggests a tactical appreciation for contemporary short attention spans. With multiple message forces, one can keep a message alive on one terrain even as it dwindles in another – a role at which blogs excel. Dead issues can reanimate: mainstream journalists report, 'bloggers are debating' or 'as was recently uncovered by blog X'. The idea of multiplying message forces highlights how messages carry affective charges. The communications strategy on which it is based doesn't turn on 'getting our message out there', as if there were to be a debate on positions that need to be understood and considered. Rather, the goal is spreading, diversifying and intensifying the message force. Abundant, dispersed, mashed up messages displace previous communication strategies focused on direct image control. Even when facts are corrected, fictions remain, repeated and circulated in affective networks. In this setting, disclosures add to the noise rather than matter as content on their own. Anything can be packaged as a secret: it's whatever I didn't know. Anything can be disclosed as a secret. Since so much circulates through the networks of communicative capitalism, previously revealed information can be presented in a new context, with a new spin, with new links, thereby becoming a new revelation.

As Tiziana Terranova expresses it, ours is an informational culture where 'meaningful experiences are under siege, continuously undermined by a proliferation of signs that have no reference, only statistical patterns of frequency, redundancy and resonance (the obsessive frequency and redundancy of an advertising campaign, the mutually reinforcing resonance of self-help manuals and expert advice, the incessant bombardment of signifying influences)'.[8]

8. Tiziana Terranova, *Network Culture: Politics for the Information Age* (New York: Pluto Press, 2005), 14.

Does Assange agree? He initially seems to. In his exchange with Goodman and Žižek, he emphasized numbers, the numbers of documents and the statistical analyses they enable. As did nearly every report on the Iraq War Logs, he announced that there were approximately 400,000 documents, that they constituted the largest stash of war documents ever published, that they provided details on over 104,000 deaths. This accentuation of the numerical attributes of the archive he's produced implies a kind of mathematical authority. Under communicative capitalism, however, an excess of polls, surveys and assessments circulates, undercutting not only the efficacy of any particular finding but the conditions of possibility for knowledge and credibility as such. There is always another analysis, done by another group or association with whatever bias and whatever methodology, displacing whatever information one thought one had. Assange also seems to think that this mathematical authority approaches something like completeness, that it can encompass the entirety of human experience, and thus provide the information that Goodman thinks is necessary for democracy. Assange explained: 'What advances us as a civilization is the entirety of our intellectual record and the entirety of our understanding about what we are going through, what human institutions are actually like and how they actually behave. And if we are to make rational policy decisions, insofar as any decision can be rational, then we have to have information that is drawn from the real world, in a description of the real world. And at the moment, we are severely lacking in the information from the interior of big secretive organizations that have such a role in shaping how civilization evolves and how we all live.'

Assange clearly shares Goodman's democratic matrix. Like her, he presupposes the possibility of undistorted, trustworthy, symbolically efficient information. Like her, he speaks as if there were no fundamental divisions or antagonism rupturing the 'public' of those who would come to know this information. Indeed, for him there is one civilization, with one record, that can be understood in its entirety. Like Goodman, Assange assumes that the withholding of such information is the barrier, the barrier that matters, to 'rational policy decision' – there are no fundamental disagreements, no class conflicts, no divisions constitutive of society as such.

Even though Assange's basic assumptions are wrong, the more interesting problem is his misunderstanding of the setting in which he operates. In presuming a closed entirety of information he fails to account for his own intervention in the communicative circuits; that is, he fails to acknowledge the fundamental reflexivity of communication. The repercussion is that he doesn't consider the amplification effects accompanying increases in the amount of information. So not only are there hundreds of thousands of new documents, analyses of these documents, reports based on these documents, and analyses and traces left whenever anyone or anything accesses the reports, documents and analyses, but there is also more commentary, more comments on the commentary, more debates on the documents, analyses, reports, commentary, and comments, and so on. This amplification thus adds to the noise of the overall environment, making it ever more difficult to focus on or access any particular item of informational content, much less understand it or galvanize activism on its basis. In adopting a conspiracy-minded conception of state power, Assange fails to grasp what the Bush administration already knew: that power in communicative capitalism relies on abundance, overkill and repetition, on the excess of information, on the way that too much information is more incapacitating than too little information (even as it enhances the feeling that there is never enough). The power of information doesn't come knowing it all; it comes from the destruction of the possibility of an all. To be clear, I am not saying that the Bush administration did not have all sorts of secrets, all sorts of information that it wanted to withhold. Rather, I am saying that the disclosure of any particular element of it, in the media setting of communicative capitalism, cannot have the sorts of political effects Assange and Goodman presume.

Guy Debord can help make this point. In his *Comments on the Society of the Spectacle*, published 20 years after *The Society of the Spectacle*,

Debord offers the notion of the 'integrated spectacle' as the highest stage of the spectacular society. Although he doesn't describe the integrated spectacle as a reflexive circuit, reflexivity is its primary conceptual innovation. Debord writes, 'For the final sense of the integrated spectacle is this – that it has integrated itself into reality to the same extent as it was describing it, and that it was reconstructing it as it was describing it. As a result, this reality no longer confronts the integrated spectacle as something alien.'[9] The integrated spectacle is an element of the world it depicts; it is part of the scene upon which it looks. When he appeals to the entirety of our understanding of what institutions are actually like, Assange neglects his place in the circuit. Differently put, he positions himself as somehow outside the system he is part of, as if it were not reflexive. This is a serious omission: since the publication of the Iraq War Logs, Assange has become the star of his own story, the centre of spectacle garnering more attention than any specific instances of 'collateral murder' in Iraq. To this extent, he displaces attention from the very political issues to which he is ostensibly trying to bring attention.

Debord misses the reflexive circuitry of the integrated spectacle because his account of the spectacle is embedded in a model of broadcast media. This is an error Assange makes as well, even as the digital networks Assange puts to use should suggest

9. Guy Debord, *Comments on the Society of the Spectacle*, trans. Malcolm Imrie (London: Verso, 1998), 9.

otherwise. His publication strategy relies on arranging for major media providers (over 80 different outlets, including major newspapers like *The Guardian*, *The New York Times*, and *Der Spiegel*) to disclose the information that has been revealed to and authenticated by WikiLeaks. Assange calls this 'co-opting' or 'leveraging' the mainstream press. The strategy makes sense for newspapers that have cut back their reporting staffs. In effect, WikiLeaks lets them outsource the journalistic work of investigative research.[10] Yet in a setting of widespread mistrust of media, it's difficult to see how Assange's content differs from other content published by the papers. Why should it be exempt from the broader scepticism towards everything else they produce? Recall, the decline of symbolic efficiency means that there is no decisive point of certainty, no shared criteria providing sure guarantees. So who is co-opting whom? Is the media co-opting Assange for free content? Is he leveraging them for more exposure? Or are they both dupes in a more complex exercise in disinformation where the CIA and the Mossad are manipulating their eagerness and credulity? Reports to this effect circulated on the Internet as early as March 2010, alleging that Asian intelligence sources believed WikiLeaks to be part of a cyber-COINTEL program: 'WikiLeaks is running a disinformation campaign, crying persecution by U.S. intelligence

10. For a more detailed account of these changes, see Felix Stalder, 'Contain This!'. First published in *Metamute* (29 November 2010). Available at http://www.eurozine.com/articles/2010-11-29-stalder-en.html.

– when it is U.S. intelligence itself.'[11]

At any rate, both Debord and Assange proceed

11. 'Is WikiLeaks a Mossad/CIA Front?', posted to Kenny's Sideshow (31 March 2010). Available at http://kennysideshow.blog-spot.com/2010/03/is-WikiLeaks-ciamossad-front.html.

as if the primary informational problem was a matter of top-down control. Debord worries that the images spectators see are 'chosen and constructed by *someone else*'.[12] When 'chosen by someone else' is the problem, the

12. Debord, *Comments*, op. cit. (note 9), 27.

solution seems like it can be found in choosing and constructing for oneself – one of the primary tenets of the hacker ethic inspiring Assange's development of WikiLeaks. Any opposition to state power appears radical, revolutionary – as if there weren't capitalists and right-wingers constantly contesting and seeking to limit the reach of state power. Assange relies on this radical aura as he positions himself as the single individual fighting *mano-a-mano* against mighty states.

Debord treats the spectacle as a form of state power insofar as the spectacle is a vehicle for control. Of course, constant, pervasive communication can also be a regime of control. That people willingly and happily disclose their views, activities, associations, and locations not only makes surveillance a lot easier but also distributes it – we stalk our friends in participatory, self-organized, control networks. Under communicative capitalism, our spectacles are the ones we make ourselves, the ones that go viral. Corporate and state power need not go

to the expense and trouble to keep people entertained, passive and diverted. They can outsource that to us under the guise of power-sharing and DIY. We do it ourselves.

Assange, though, perceives contemporary governance as authoritarian because it relies on secrets, integrating members into a shared conspiracy. His view resonates here with Debord's claim that 'generalized secrecy stands behind the spectacle, as the decisive complement of all it displays and, in the last analysis its most vital operation'.[13] In writings from 2006, Assange treats

13. Ibid., 12.

conspiracy as a mode of governance, arguing that secrets form the heart of authoritarian power. He writes: 'Since unjust systems, by their nature induce opponents, and in many places barely have the upper hand, mass leaking leaves them exquisitely vulnerable to those who seek to replace them with more open forms of governance.'[14] Assange does not consider that open forms of governance can also be unjust, that revelation, data-dumping and message force

14. Julian Assange, 'The non-linear effects of leaks on unjust systems of governance', posted to the iq.org (31 December 2006). Available at http://web.archive.org/web/20071020051936/http://iq.org/#Thenonlineareffectsofleaksonunjustsystemsofgovernance.

multipliers can and do serve as tactics in networked information war. More information can entail more diversion from central lines of antagonism, more dispersion of political energies.

The conviction that power requires secrecy may also explain Assange's own penchant for secrecy. As Geert Lovink and Patrice Riemans point out, Assange defends the lack of transparency in the WikiLeaks organization by saying that it 'needs to be completely opaque in order to force others to be totally transparent'.[15] Despite the apparent irony of a secret organization fighting for more open governance, Assange remains firmly within the democratic matrix. Because he thinks of conspiracy as the mode of governance in authoritarian regimes, he views revelation and concealment as primary tactics in political struggle. Yet insofar as he fails to look beyond the democratic matrix, he misses the changes in their operation. Because communicative capitalism's media setting is open, distributive, recombinant and chaotic, revelation is much less effective than repetition and much less disruptive than tactics that focus on political goals beyond media exposure.

I conclude by turning to remarks by the third participant in the discussion, Žižek. Pointing out that much of the content that WikiLeaks leaks is already known, Žižek argued that WikiLeaks is nonetheless a radical threat to the formal functioning of power. He explained that: 'The real disturbance was at the level of appearances: we can no longer pretend we don't know what everyone knows we know. This is the paradox of public space: even if everyone knows an unpleasant fact, saying it in public changes everything.' The problem with Žižek's point is that 'saying' had already occurred. In other words,

15. Geert Lovink and Patrice Riemans, 'Twelve Theses on WikiLeaks', *Eurozine* (7 December 2010). Available at http://www.eurozine.com/articles/2010-12-07-lovink-riemens-en.html.

Žižek begins with the concession that much of what was reported was not new; it was already known. This means that it had already been reported, already been said, and yet this saying didn't disturb the level of appearances at all. And the reason it didn't disturb the level of appearances is that this level doesn't exist. The decline of symbolic efficiency means that there isn't a public sphere of accepted truths and rules of the game. On the contrary, as the Bush administration's tactics in info-war already make clear, the milieu of communicative capitalism is fragmented, uneven, reflective and dispersed.

Now one might rightfully object that if my analysis here is correct why is Bradley Manning in prison? Doesn't that suggest that WikiLeaks threatens state power? It seems to me that it's Manning and other leakers who present threats to power. But this isn't new: soldiers who violate military rules always face severe charges. Those who reveal state secrets are already treated severely. Could it be, then, that WikiLeaks threatens the structure of power by arming and protecting leakers, by given them opportunities to share previously secret information that before they would have been unable to distribute even if they wanted to? Only if one assumes that secrecy is the heart of power. If, however, one recognizes the changed media setting of communicative capitalism, one that thrives on the multiplication and replication and circulation of information and commentary in fast, ubiquitous networks that distract and disperse us, then WikiLeaks is just another spectacular hub.

In his *London Review of Books* piece on WikiLeaks, Žižek writes: 'The aim of the WikiLeaks revelations was not just to embarrass those in power but to lead us to mobilize ourselves to bring about a different functioning of power that might reach beyond the limits of representative democracy.'[16] If Žižek is right, then WikiLeaks aimed to incite action, widespread action, outside and against the US government. Instead, WikiLeaks displaced the little focused opposition to the war that remained back onto itself. Rather than mobilizing people, WikiLeaks offers Assange as a surrogate into which we can invest our fantasies of action… before we click on some other links and watch some other videos on YouTube.

16. Slavoj Žižek, 'Good Manners in the Age of WikiLeaks', *London Review of Books* vol. 33, no. 2 (20 January 2011), 9-10.

```
90 9A 5C EF FB 39 22 B1 73 6A 35 07 5B BB BD 79
C1 BF ED 0F 81 0C 29 95 29 6F 27 50 B3 E7 C6 9B
D4 DA F8 67 93 96 0E 95 EA ED 3B 19 98 31 B6 A9
E9 33 00 9C 5B 07 95 65 AE E2 AD F9 F5 43 BE 9C
2B E2 50 43 E5 93 9F A6 7F 47 D2 DD C9 27 86 ED
8A F1 5E 06 08 2B ED C1 A9 22 50 BD A5 D3 68 E5
D5 3C 1B 03 1A FC F2 1A 44 3B 78 31 23 E2 39 EF
67 C3 B7 9B 27 D1 CA 49 8D B7 A2 DC 54 7D 4C 70
A7 83 BF E9 E0 B6 97 72 2F 49 BC 9B A6 A1 07 45
E3 46 D8 EA 1A E3 8F 0D 77 E1 70 68 C2 1E BE 6C
02 02 15 14 D8 46 B1 4E A6 2D 84 DA AE 54 18 BE
B5 FF F6 53 9D 7A 10 00 F8 59 E0 33 3C 5F B9 43
94 02 74 57 21 E7 7F E1 61 81 EC 8C 09 43 F2 36
27 C8 EC 2C 53 0C 81 6F BA 63 38 68 18 7E F4 22
65 29 9A 4D AF 00 F4 41 02 4E 7B 4B 97 01 42 58
6E 4B 44 1F F5 4E 5A 61 7D 90 3B 69 86 5E A2 16
1B F6 70 CD CD 11 B2 93 EB 8D F0 E2 1F 0C 59 1A
73 88 D1 BB 87 B2 E2 4B A1 3A DC B4 B3 E2 68 81
C9 4C 91 09 9C 5C 1C D7 41 01 FF 94 2E C8 A6 68
55 E2 77 77 56 C4 9A 45 E1 56 C5 D8 7B 23 7C 75
3A BC 6D 87 CE 28 42 5E 80 7C 50 B3 6F 37 4A 18
92 83 E8 8D 7A E9 A5 CD 26 8D 15 93 CC 61 36 53
EE 0D 28 3D F8 F7 DE 28 50 C9 C0 9E D6 FB 04 33
C7 1E FD DB EE 3A E5 58 5E 60 4E 48 49 CE B4 CA
2A 41 7E 19 C7 DF F5 0F 09 4B 5C 58 E8 90 E6 03
AF BD E5 02 52 1E B5 B5 2F 96 BE 53 1B B2 F1 A1
82 A7 F0 13 DE CE F1 B9 D1 C6 5F 6A 64 15 8E A9
8D 0F 5E D1 E4 D3 75 C1 F4 FF 84 0E 33 6E 17 B3
95 3D 5A 96 C8 63 45 68 CD 2C 6E FF B1 F0 8C 90
4B B8 06 5A 7C 5D F9 95 0E 18 B2 A8 55 C5 6C 2B
FD 4C 9D B7 28 02 29 3B 26 B3 F4 C9 16 F9 CB BB
D6 D9 6C 31 E7 4A BC EA A3 F2 E4 AC E5 51 CE F3
82 5F 1A 79 CA 8E 3E F0 81 54 8A AB 76 F1 7D F7
21 91 68 F7 93 49 D7 7A 9F 56 F6 F5 BC DE BA AB
8F 85 D2 CD E0 16 EF BF 64 91 EE 82 81 54 C8 00
10 F2 60 30 24 DF 45 E0 1E E1 59 D8 42 26 3E D5
E5 99 DB 02 AE B8 0A DC 6F 25 3D 47 D8 F8 9E 8E
26 7E C2 A5 13 F5 40 FE 4B 9C D9 CF D7 BA 1C A5
04 3F 69 DF DE F5 D7 27 82 3E 53 15 CB 6A 5C CB
1E 82 AE 1E 2E 4B 39 83 55 30 82 4E 8A 08 50 B4
6A 81 09 0B 10 03 95 59 93 A8 1C 06 EE 34 AC C1
F3 1E 3E 9E 9E FE 39 C9 EA 81 2B 7F 37 AF 8C D6
36 7D 99 73 3C ED 7F 66 39 4F 5D EC 89 18 B2 45
F6 4A 37 17 B1 2B 93 57 77 C1 C0 2A CB 97 C6 94
F6 70 3B D1 85 A1 6D 4E F2 79 AF CE 7B 19 9D 3C
5C 1B D2 49 FE 33 C1 28 0D 8A D9 81 06 E3 4E B9
71 1B A8 13 D4 E3 6D 0D A9 5B B5 60 1F 6F A7 0C
38 47 FB 1D 7D AD 3B 44 77 AF 21 BB AE 5E BB 39
69 30 4C 9C 0F 1E CF 98 CF A8 1D CD 1F 3B ED A2
```

```
0C  6C  1D  AA  93  28  D6  7B  02  8C  89  D7  48  EF  CB  CC
A4  32  C1  9F  40  53  F6  73  0C  4F  13  C9  60  E2  BA  B0
CE  55  F6  6A  3A  BD  A1  B3  33  F4  27  45  13  AD  22  75
EE  01  1B  2D  8B  08  69  11  D2  AC  56  30  09  C1  B2  6A
72  51  5B  45  11  41  BE  A9  59  7B  4A  BF  4B  CA  41  56
6F  BE  DA  61  A7  43  06  0C  5C  AD  82  D0  0E  2A  CE  CD
B6  53  5B  BC  DE  3B  35  F2  2A  72  3C  1C  2A  78  C0  05
91  E7  D5  E5  AA  08  15  B5  D2  8D  7D  90  11  EC  9B  EE
E2  1C  F6  14  B5  EC  00  C2  0D  6C  8E  29  EB  7A  7C  55
2B  C0  E1  40  D8  7A  74  A5  18  5C  C4  49  75  84  41  F7
5B  A1  B2  63  03  84  B3  45  F1  74  A1  64  1D  28  D2  E0
B6  AA  64  A6  B6  65  5F  DF  76  D9  0C  42  3B  76  3B  96
81  EB  D1  44  15  90  27  DF  80  EA  2E  32  A9  80  A3  95
8E  59  8D  A9  43  EC  CC  21  3D  7C  DC  BC  7E  D5  5C  AB
22  2C  06  47  77  5B  13  A0  4C  F9  1B  2F  40  5F  92  EF
4A  90  F0  11  0A  AA  49  85  07  71  4E  CC  1A  0A  11  27
74  38  35  CF  A1  74  31  73  B0  7A  04  E3  81  0B  65  DF
2F  C9  93  C8  C9  51  9D  CD  55  A3  76  AA  59  02  F8  FA
7D  97  03  E0  07  6B  0D  9B  FA  57  9B  10  E8  7E  D2  62
C2  82  1B  69  BA  FB  46  D5  DB  20  AB  57  57  9B  CE  DD
76  82  6D  C7  F5  1E  59  FF  9E  C0  B9  00  85  21  86  B6
5F  1C  04  23  DE  AD  79  0A  38  78  E6  17  1C  BA  E6  FD
E6  C0  62  3A  D2  B3  63  3A  15  6C  DF  86  64  5B  50  45
D6  52  52  9F  79  3F  1B  5D  79  95  3F  0D  86  17  8B  F1
BA  2C  11  B4  2B  87  30  27  A7  3C  2E  5B  FA  AE  D7  67
3F  25  30  ED  FA  F4  BE  36  64  68  59  6A  70  E6  C1  85
DA  08  47  13  1B  27  C8  66  7B  50  B5  BB  4D  A0  6D  73
01  BD  34  17  B0  EB  1B  7A  E8  6F  34  93  73  28  41  18
41  AF  C8  C0  02  0A  9B  6E  D8  BD  2A  12  01  4C  18  67
F2  12  DF  D8  17  B9  87  BE  78  51  A3  BE  88  09  B8  DF
27  32  9F  5C  96  A9  F9  66  2A  9F  4E  3B  62  E7  06  CB
4C  9E  1C  22  51  0A  98  65  6E  75  58  48  6B  D5  54  6C
95  14  F7  58  55  61  A4  25  26  FB  4D  B0  65  D2  51  87
91  7F  96  7B  42  C9  E9  61  AD  CB  AE  A7  50  21  90  C5
8E  B6  18  E0  F3  76  C8  34  3C  86  AC  01  AF  61  68  F8
A2  EC  D0  36  DE  7F  E8  C5  2B  4A  EA  E1  8E  2D  EE  B7
40  E8  5D  B8  50  D4  B5  7B  FC  7E  F7  4A  BF  E9  5C  58
CA  A3  CD  69  61  69  DE  AB  97  60  01  93  6C  6D  59  49
7F  C7  0D  26  C3  E6  ED  04  EA  BA  FA  7F  A6  F2  BF  FE
C6  C9  3E  79  73  A6  1A  58  A4  F2  E7  45  B9  C0  1F  7D
A4  3E  5F  F0  DC  E4  51  F5  B7  93  FA  B7  B5  0C  65  F8
02  12  08  EB  34  47  51  8B  1A  BD  59  60  16  99  69  F3
28  3F  03  83  5D  63  34  41  D3  1E  C8  0D  E7  BF  0E  13
BC  4C  07  D9  B0  C5  93  0C  DB  EF  AF  E2  7D  6A  B3  87
8F  AE  B6  9C  9E  DA  01  40  D7  3D  6E  F0  36  9D  13  3E
68  05  48  F5  2C  2C  2E  32  5D  AC  AF  EF  F3  0D  4F  29
1A  74  CC  58  8E  A1  2D  8D  10  5B  F1  E6  6A  2E  76  31
12  DE  25  39  DC  27  5D  8F  B4  3A  D5  61  C5  56  73  12
D3  17  E9  AD  D2  34  82  86  95  A0  6B  96  84  F7  28  4E
```

column

TRANSPARENCY AS CULT
WIKILEAKS AND FACEBOOK

JORINDE SEIJDEL

In the light of a critical examination of today's transparency ideologies, comparing Facebook and WikiLeaks with each other in a basic manner is surprisingly clarifying. At first, this might seem inappropriate, because of the apparently fundamentally different premises and divergent social, economic and political views of these super-topical digital platforms: Facebook as an ultra-capitalistic billion-dollar company versus WikiLeaks as an activist, non-profit organization; Facebook as a social network for the exchange of personal information versus WikiLeaks as a whistle-blower site for anonymous revelations of public interest; Facebook as commercial purloiner and trader of information versus WikiLeaks as altruistic provider of information.

There are also many similarities, however: both Facebook and WikiLeaks are to a large degree products of an increased societal desire for disclosure. Both seek their societal legitimization in the philosophy (or doctrine) of transparency and the sharing of information, and on the basis of that, both preach a better world – whereby 'Julian Assange sees the world as filled with real and imagined enemies; Zuckerberg sees the world as filled with potential friends', as *Time Magazine* once put it. In their fanatical creed of transparency, both organizations have also been accused of serious violations of people's privacy (despite WikiLeaks' position that transparency is something for government and not for individuals), while both Zuckerberg and Assange seem to actually encourage a certain mystification as regards their own person. Last but not least, both claim a significant role as stoker of the revolutions in the Middle East. In that regard, however, Assange, who considers WikiLeaks a check on power, called Facebook an 'appalling spy machine' for the American government and its intelligence services. Zuckerberg, on the other hand, does see ideological similarities 'somewhere': 'At a higher level some of the themes may be connected.'

Be that as it may, somewhere in the shining clarity of radical transparency there is an acute black hole, a dark spot where Facebook and WikiLeaks meet. The question is: At that frightful point of convergence, what happens with the first resumed differences? Are they confirmed after a fleeting contact, so that a process of semantic and ideological divergence can immediately resume, or might it be revealed that these podiums indeed both are a special kind of 'service', proceeding from their dedication to transparency? And then here the word 'service' is also meant in the sense of 'celebration' or 'cult'. But who or what is being served, and if this is a cult, what is being worshiped or celebrated?

At first sight, of course, this seems to be a cult of visibility, whereby Facebook and WikiLeaks, in their craving for universality, complement one another as counterparts: the former involves the 'community' in the celebration and the latter its institutes; both must be transparent. In this immense transparent bliss, the communal is then celebrated and claimed, as one big discourse and a democratic exchange, whereby an immaterial, intangible service is provided to the *populus*, a service that it carries out itself, as a higher specimen of Do-It-Yourself. DIY in the sense that it is the 'populist body' itself that produces (by sharing and by publishing) the experience of transparency and *communis*, which it then digests and consumes.

So in fact, the communal is also what is 'drawn up' and offered in this cult, and what disappears into the all-absorbing black hole of hyper-transparency. And so this concerns a service to visibility and openness just as much as to secrecy. The core of the communal and public can thus never be situated purely in the visible and transparent, but is equally present in the hidden and opaque. (In this light, it is under-standable that the central focus in the new reality programmes, such as *Secret Story*, is on keeping a secret, instead of exacting extreme transparency from the participants.)

Thus the contrived search for a point of convergence between Facebook and WikiLeaks as a small thought experiment at any rate results in the realization that, despite their differing ideologies and objectives, the paradigms underlying these two organizations are not essentially different. On the contrary, it is precisely together that they manifest the dominant paradigm to which the demand for transparency belongs *in optima forma*. They equally well demonstrate together, as counterparts of one another, that the philosophy of transparency and its logistic or performative system not only makes the communal visible but also makes it evaporate and lets it escape.

Willem van Weelden

WikiLeaks as an Editorial Problem

A Conversation with Geert Lovink and Merijn Oudenampsen

In the wake of the developments around WikiLeaks, the time is ripe to take a closer look at the current information landscape. Willem van Weelden, researcher and publicist specialized in media and culture, spoke with political sociologist Merijn Oudenampsen and media theorist Geert Lovink on how WikiLeaks can effect social and political change and contribute to making power more transparent.

Questions of censorship, information filtering and ideologically coloured news services seem to have entered a new phase: Facebook's filtering of data flows generated by the Arab Spring in order to prevent existing regimes from misusing information; censorship of the regular media in the USA as a result of the WikiLeaks revelations; extreme sanctions imposed by the Chinese government against internal dissident voices; growing populism in Europe, urging greater state control over the media and more transparent policy; the illegal wiretapping practices of Rupert Murdoch's bungling media empire, which became the victim of overplaying its own hand . . .

These almost arbitrary examples point to a general change of climate in news coverage and pose the question of what the term 'media ecology' could still mean. Or, to reformulate the question in a cybernetic and thus almost politically neutral fashion: What is the connecting pattern that emerges in this hybrid constellation of mutually influencing factors? The answer can only be discovered through a network analysis and a political/aesthetic analysis of ideology and editing, (informational) power and spheres of influence. We can then perhaps say that the first lesson that WikiLeaks has thoroughly impressed upon the world reintroduces what in principle is an old fact: namely, that exposing the way in which data and information is handled is – painfully enough – more revealing than the possibly extremely compromising content of the 'hard data' itself. The ultimate consequence of this conclusion goes much further than the almost pathetic battles Julian Assange believes he must wage in order to preserve 'the truth'. In that respect, let us above all not forget that 'truth' is a media effect that is produced! With its cleverly directed, media-savvy campaigns, WikiLeaks seems to be following the same logic that lies at the bottom of the escapades of the distressed Murdoch empire.

Assange's media logic became almost palpable when he stated in an interview with Amy Goodman and in conversation with the philosopher Slavoj Žižek on the American radio show *Democracy Now* that he was amazed by the fact that the populist and nationalistic Fox News show had shown more images of the shocking *Collateral Murder* video than had CNN, which at the first hail of bullets had broadcasted a blank screen under the pretext that it wanted to spare the families of the victims.[1] Assange assumed that despite the fact that Fox had condemned WikiLeak's publication of the video

1. Broadcast on 12 July 2011.

images and treated the material in a biased and tendentious manner, the truth was more served by Fox than by the prudish CNN. Assange's 'truth' appears to be a videographic truth, an almost transparent ideology of media penetration. It is precisely this aspect of the Assange doctrine that has evoked the requisite restraint and reserve in a camp that one would normally expect to have supported him – the leftist-activist camp.

How can we arrive at a correct assessment of all the different levels and scales of importance connected with WikiLeaks and subsequently construct a truly productive framework of action? With this splintering of perspectives, what is necessary in order to find an answer that not only unites but also spurs democratic action, and offers a counterbalance to the imminent threats created by the exponential increase of control over historiography, access to information, freedom of speech, freedom of movement, freedom of dissidence and freedom of questioning? What does WikiLeaks have to offer within this subversive framework?

The leftist camp is divided on WikiLeaks as an activist phenomenon and has a hard time properly interpreting its effects. On the one hand, there is mistrust of front man Julian Assange, who according to some has emerged as a dictatorial leader and self-styled celebrity who has piloted WikiLeaks into populist waters. On the other hand, with the publication of hundreds of thousands of documents, the WikiLeaks motto 'No power without accountability' has unleashed an undeniable force and caused an inspiring chaos in geopolitical relations. At the same time, WikiLeaks' impact on the regular news media can hardly be underestimated.

In any case, WikiLeaks always knows how to take advantage of a momentum and capture global attention with new revelations, as witnessed not only by the shocking images of *Collateral Murder*, but also by the publication of a tremendous amount of documents on the wars in Iraq and Afghanistan, the 779 documents on the American detention camp Guantánamo, the hundreds of files on the crisis areas of Honduras and Pakistan, and of course the very extensive collection of diplomatic documents (the 'cable files'). Time and again, WikiLeaks has caused consternation and desperation on the side of the people, parties and institutions compromised by the revelations.

Yet these revelations, no matter how shocking and historically important, do not seem to be the only merit of WikiLeaks: it has above all demonstrated that an anarchistic way of dealing with reporting is a public good and can generate democratic effects. In order to effectuate this, WikiLeaks has moreover installed a 'custom-made' infrastructure. In short, WikiLeaks is only the beginning of a promise. To quote the conservative thinker Oliver Wendell Holmes: 'The mind, once expanded to the dimensions of larger ideas, never returns to its original size.'

What To Do?

So far, the fiercest reaction to WikiLeaks has been in the USA, which is not strange when you consider that the platform appears to be waging an emphatic information war against the goings-on of what still may be regarded as one of the most powerful countries in the world. That its power is at stake due to the revelations made by WikiLeaks is evidenced by the reactions, which have varied from calls for legal action and the freezing of WikiLeaks' assets – which have indeed occurred – to repeated exhortations for Assange's sentencing and execution.

WikiLeaks has received support, in itself not surprising, from the hactivist collective Anonymous, which reacted with DdoS (Distributed Denial of Service) attacks on credit card companies that had frozen WikiLeaks' assets (Maestro and PayPal) and additionally devoted themselves to 'Operation Crowdleaks': an attempt with the help of volunteers to translate collective information provided by WikiLeaks for a larger audience. The tactic behind this form of mass journalism is to publish cables that thus far have had little or no attention in the media. In the meantime, WikiLeaks and Assange have received various awards, including the Amnesty International UK Media Award. Slavoj Žižek has expressed himself positively about WikiLeaks and Assange's fight; while Daniel Ellsberg, who in the book *Pentagon Papers* leaked information in the 1970s on the war in Vietnam, has meanwhile been exerting himself on countless forums to draw parallels between how he was assailed as a whistle-blower at the time and the way in which Assange has been thwarted and prosecuted in America by both the government and corporations.

Perhaps less obvious is the support that WikiLeaks has received from the art world. Less obvious because, as the account of former WikiLeaks coworker Daniel Domscheit-Berg demonstrates, Assange's attitude towards art is, to put it mildly, rather reserved.[2] The question of the extent to which WikiLeaks could benefit from art, or vice versa, is closely connected to the general question of how the WikiLeaks strategy relates to global developments and power relations, and how it can contribute to the rediscovery of a perspective for social and cultural action and emancipation.

2. Daniel Domscheit-Berg, *Inside WikiLeaks* (Amsterdam: Lebowski Publishers, 2011).

In the following conversation with Geert Lovink, media theorist and founder of the Institute of Network Cultures, and Merijn Oudenampsen, political scientist and sociologist, both also allied with different generations of hackers and activists, the dilemmas outlined above come to the fore in varying contexts. Lovink and Oudenampsen contributed greatly to a public discussion conducted both online and offline about WikiLeaks, sometimes seemingly taking different standpoints. In December 2010, Lovink co-authored with Patrice Riemens a polemic piece about WikiLeaks, called 'Twelve Theses on WikiLeaks', which appeared in various European papers and online forums. It was published in the Dutch newspaper *NRC Handelsblad* under the heading 'Voor WikiLeaks telt alleen de banaliteit van het spektakel' (All That Counts for WikiLeaks is the Banality of the Spectacle). Oudenampsen reacted fiercely to this piece through the *Nettime* mailing list with the article *12 Stellingen, 13 ongelukken* (12 Theses, 13 Disasters).[3]

3. For Lovink and Riemens' text, see: digitaleeditie.nrc.nl/digitaleeditie/NH/2010/11/20101211___/2_01/article1.html www.eurozine.com/articles/2010-12-07-lovinkriemens-en.html. For Oudenampsen's reaction, see: www.nettime.org/Lists-Archives/nettime-nl-1012/msg00020.html.

This conversation modifies their differences of opinion somewhat and contains no incontrovertible statements or detailed solutions. Starting from the phenomenon of WikiLeaks, it explores where there is room for social and political change and where there are perspectives that can contribute to greater transparency of the workings of power.

Willem van Weelden: *In his article 'Transparency and Exodus: On Political Process in the Mediated Democracies', the cultural critic Brian Holmes quotes Felix Guattari: 'What is it that separates the left from the right? . . . Fundamentally, it is nothing but a processual calling, a processual passion [author's italics – ed.].'[4] Holmes draws a parallel between certain forms of activism and experimental art: both are said to have a processual character in that they resist stereotyping, pigeonholing and unequivocal left/right divisions of the political power arena.*

4. Brian Holmes, 'Transparency and Exodus: On Political Process in the Mediated Democracies', *Open: Cahier on Art and the Public Domain*, no. 8 '(In)Visibility: Beyond the Image in Art, Culture and the Public Domain' (Amsterdam/Rotterdam: SKOR/NAi Publishers, 2005), 49.

What about the left wing's passion with respect to WikiLeaks? In the discussions on WikiLeaks, the two of you initially seem to be diametrically opposed when it comes to a critical interpretation. All the same, the content and process of WikiLeaks has been less in the news lately. The media's attention skips from an item on Assange's behaviour to the next scandal about the peripheral symptoms of the phenomenon. This raises the question of the extent to which the alternative camp is still capable of not only putting Holmes's celebrated processual passion on the agenda concerning WikiLeaks, but also successfully implementing it.

Merijn Oudenampsen: I think WikiLeaks gives visibility to the filtering process in the traditional media, and that there has been a strategy, if not a tactic, of publicizing the WikiLeaks narrative in a particular manner. By focusing on the personage of Assange, the spectacle, the stories about Gaddafi's bodyguard, the character of Sarkozy or – as happened in the Dutch paper *NRC Handelsblad* – by discussing the literary qualities of the cables, it was possible to avoid dealing with the more fundamental issues in terms of content. On the one hand, this would seem to point to lazy journalism (as is often the case in the Netherlands). On the other, it could also have been the result of a conscious strategy, such as with *The New York Times,* whose editors met with bureaucrats from Washington in order to decide what to publish and what not. Afterward, a cable downplaying the threat of the Iranian rocket programme was purposely not published, while an article with an opposite slant was put out. This sort of case is a typical illustration of Noam Chomsky's classical position on the functioning of Western media as a mouthpiece of the established order. That is certainly true for the USA, but in the Netherlands you don't immediately expect it.

WvW: *At the time, you criticized the publication of Patrice Riemens and Geert Lovink's text in* NRC Handelsblad. *Was the choice of* NRC Handelsblad *as a platform the most important point of criticism for you? After all, this paper took a rather conservative stance on WikiLeaks.*

MO: In the first instance I was shocked by the headline, 'All That Counts for WikiLeaks is the Banality of the Spectacle'. However, that turned out to be formulated by the paper itself, not written by Geert and Patrice. I was indeed concerned about the context in which the piece appeared: in the Dutch media, including the *NRC*, WikiLeaks was attacked as being irresponsible and Assange was set aside as an eccentric figure with megalomania. Of all places, the article appeared in this context, and then written by people whom you would expect to stand up for WikiLeaks; but that didn't happen. At least, that's the impression it gave, also because the *NRC* had omitted Lovink and Riemens' first thesis (the zero thesis: 'WikiLeaks is a good thing'). Geert and Patrice had originally written the text for the online mailing list *Nettime* with the intention of it being a critical piece. In the context of the *NRC*, it did not have that effect. This is why I thought it would be good to thoroughly examine precisely this point in the discussion that unfolded on *Nettime*. Judging from the reactions I received, there actually turned out to be little sympathy for this. I think that's strange. After all, *Nettime* is part of a world that ought to have sympathy for something like WikiLeaks. Where was it? I absolutely cannot explain that. But after all, I'm from a different generation.

Geert Lovink: I have indeed moved beyond Chomsky's criticism from the early 1980s, although it has lost nothing of its validity. In working with activists and artists, it is good to repeat that criticism from time to time, but it no longer generates any new strategies. So I don't have a problem with its veracity, but with its effect on the creativity of collective subversion. It curtails the many possibilities that there are. Very concretely, the filtering of information always makes me think of processes that take place at the *NRC* or *The New York Times*, which are clear to me. But a book has just come out by Eli Pariser that discusses new forms of power generated by very fine filtering processes that offer personalized information to users of Google, Facebook and other information distributors without their really being aware of it.[5] These are developments that could truly lead to new insights into how the media powers of the twenty-first century work. They no longer work by manipulation from

5. Eli Pariser, *The Filter Bubble: What the Internet is Hiding from You* (New York: The Penguin Press, 2011).

the top down, but by giving people the feeling that they are being served and can develop themselves, that they are being taken seriously and their subject is being addressed. With information filtering, I see new workings of power; and I am extremely curious about this because I think that new activist strategies should above all focus on that. We've known for a while now that the *NRC* and other old media manipulate and have a certain agenda.

Engaged Art and the Journey Out of the Reservation

WvW: *It is striking that it is above all artists who are reacting to WikiLeaks in an interesting manner, while this is much less the case with regular activists. Merijn, you have expressed rather critical views on engaged art, for example in your reaction to the essay by the artist Jonas Staal,* Post-propaganda.[6] *To what extent do you feel that the art world's support of WikiLeaks is interesting or important for the further propagation of the transparency agenda? Assange himself seems to have a tremendous disdain for art, according to the book by former WikiLeaks co-worker Daniel Domscheit-Berg.*[7]

6. Jonas Staal, *Post-propaganda* (Amsterdam: Fonds BKVB, 2009).

7. Domscheit-Berg, *Inside WikiLeaks*, op. cit. (note 2).

MO: My criticism of Jonas Staal arose from the discussion about the so-called 'new engaged art' in the Netherlands. This new engagement surprises me because it doesn't take any position at all. Jonas Staal, whose art is considered part of this movement, is someone who represents social contradictions in his work, but does not take a position himself. And that's called the new engagement. The old engagement was about intellectuals and writers taking a position, like Zola's *J'Accuse* with the Dreyfus affair. With Sartre, the existential notion of engagement involved a moral responsibility whereby it was impossible not to take a position, because aloofness is also a position.[8] And now you end up with a form of new engagement that in fact means interaction, it's about art that engages with the public. This notion of engagement as interactive art was pushed forward under Tony Blair as the spearhead of the cultural policy of New Labour, a vision that was later supported by Richard Florida with his book on the creative industry.[9] If that's the new engagement, then the old notion of the term utterly escapes me. My criticism of Staal was formulated on the basis of this difference, because in the Netherlands there is hardly any engaged art at all!

8. Jean-Paul Sartre, *Being and Nothingness: A Phenomenological Essay on Ontology* (London: Taylor & Francis, 1956).

9. Richard Florida, *The Rise of the Creative Class* (Cambridge, MA: Basic Books, 2002).

For the rest, specific identities like artist and activist don't interest me that much. I think more in terms of a series of skills, a repertoire of competencies that enable people to examine a social reality in a totally different manner, to undermine existing perspectives, to stimulate people to a new kind of reflexivity. . . . Activism is often more aimed at effect, at presentation on the streets, at making a claim based on a certain identity, while art can actually question such claims. I think that examining and questioning is very interesting at the moment, because in the case of WikiLeaks it's not possible to make a very clear claim.

WvW: *But was Brian Holmes right in saying that there are parallels between activism and art, and that they now are very obviously visible? Or is it so that we can no longer identify a phenomenon such as WikiLeaks and its spectacular actions as activism?*

MO: It is most certainly activism, and I think that there are also parallels with art – just not in the Netherlands. The Netherlands has a very strong tradition of depoliticization and of what Jacques Rancière calls the logic of 'police': compartmentalization, or pigeonholing.[10] You're in the literary world, or you're in the new media world, etcetera. Everybody's got their own sandbox to play in. The point of all art that is engaged is to 'get out of the reservation', as the philosopher and writer Jacq Vogelaar says. That's just been put on the agenda again.

10. Jacques Rancière, *Disagreement: Politics and Philosophy* (Minneapolis: University of Minnesota Press, 1999).

GL: That's because the reservations are being dismantled!

MO: Yes, the zoos are being torn down, the gates thrown open, and they're not feeding the animals anymore! But from an international point of view, there is certainly a question of convergence. I think this is because the activist identity, the certitude of being a worker or a squatter, for example, no longer exists. Such identity frameworks have disappeared. So lots of activists have acquired the same investigative attitude as artists. They understand one another much better now.

GL: The problem is that the process of political awakening is no longer occurring gradually. Everywhere, 'waking up' is taking the form of gigantic eruptions. Revolts, uprisings, resistance, or whatever you want to call them, are no longer the consequence of political organization per se. At the most, you could say that a political organization comes forth from it. That may also be true of what is happening right now in the Middle East. And that's also why we are so focused on the so-called Facebook revolutions, not because those uprisings are the result of Facebook, but because we do not understand how such political eruptions come about. For it is abundantly clear that they no longer are the result of a cumulative growth of political organization.

You could also question the extent to which these eruptions are the result of alienation, of great despair, such as was the case in Spain and Greece, or with the smaller eruptions in Italy. With change, I primarily think of that effect, whereby the logic of being shut away in a reservation of your own is radically shattered.

WvW: *Does the tearing down of those old pigeonholes and reservations produce an effect of transparency? The Arab Spring became famous because the social media supposedly had a corrective effect on dictatorial power, and so forth, but at the same time it must be said that those very media also made it much easier to pick up dissidents. Could you say that, in parallel to the transparency movement, WikiLeaks has manoeuvred itself into the position of an International Tribunal of abuses and faulty practices? And that in doing so, they place themselves outside the legal frameworks?*

MO: I don't think it's anywhere near that bad. What WikiLeaks has released doesn't even fall under the category of 'top secret'. But Ellsberg's *Pentagon Papers*, which revealed the cynical politics behind the Vietnam War, were top secret at one time. Ellsberg is the man who so many years later is seen as a great model and defender of democracy, certainly within the Democratic Party. It is remarkable to see that WikiLeaks, on the basis of releasing much less important documents, is now branded as a semi-terrorist organization. That says a lot about the spirit of the times. The Democrats also don't have any regard for WikiLeaks, while the newspapers who once published the *Pentagon Papers* are now spoon-fed by Washington. For that matter, WikiLeaks plays a modest role that we must not exaggerate. I find Assange's claim that WikiLeaks made the uprisings in the Middle East possible rather arrogant.

GL: The release of the *Pentagon Papers* took place at the height of the anti-war movement, anti-Vietnam and very many other movements in the late 1960s, early 1970s. It's almost impossible to see those things separately from one another. At this moment in time, what social context should we place WikiLeaks in? Looking back, I would think that WikiLeaks is connected not so much to social movements, but to the major events that occurred during the period of the financial crisis of 2008-2009, which caused the erosion of capitalist legitimacy.

WvW: *So, then, do you also agree with Assange, as he cites in the* e-flux *interview with Hans Ulrich Obrist, that power is increasingly located outside governmental circles and can be found in patronage, the lobbies of the banks, the stock market and the big corporations, and that the most important decisions are made there?* [11] *Do you share his analysis that this constellation cannot be controlled within the*

11. See *e-flux journal* nos. 25 and 26 for the Hans Ulrich Obrist's two-part interview with Assange: www.e-flux.com/journal.

traditional frameworks and that it should be made transparent in an alternative manner?

GL: Yes, but I think that WikiLeaks is only a start at making those lobbying and consultation structures transparent. I think it would be good if things developed more in that direction. In the Netherlands, the construction fraud whistle-blower is still undertaking legal action in order to gain recognition for what he did.[12] So here, too, we are only at the beginning of the process of making power transparent. WikiLeaks and comparable initiatives play a big role in this. An important question is what we could do to facilitate that process.

12. Ad Bos, a Dutch contractor who primarily is known as the whistle-blower in the so-called building fraud affair. In 1998, he discovered duplicate accounts held by his employer, the Koop Tjuchem construction firm, and made them public. See: nl.wikipedia.org/wiki/Ad_Bos.

Transparency and Media Strategy

MO: That's a fascinating point. The spectacle that Geert refers to in 'Twelve Theses' seems to form an inherent part of getting into newspapers like *The New York Times*, *Der Spiegel*, *The Guardian*, and so forth. Within the American publicity world, a great deal is known about what goes on behind the closed doors of Goldman Sachs, the relation between Goldman Sachs and the political-financial elite, or other abuses within the financial world, but in one way or another, the news coverage on this is never mainstream. I find that contradiction interesting: the spectacle or the personalization is precisely what makes it possible for WikiLeaks to get through to the mainstream.

GL: That's also a difficulty. On the one hand, I see the efforts of WikiLeaks from the perspective of hackers, and how they have become a productive part of facilitating openness, and on the other from the perspective of the crisis of investigative and quality journalism in general. Can we indeed gamble that if you have quality in that area, it will also lead to a political reversal? It turns out that personalization is one of the crucial facilitating factors. I have problems with that, because if you bet on celebrity strategy instead of the quality of the work, of diligently seeking out the precise workings of power and describing them, then a lot gets lost. That's the dilemma we're facing right now.

WvW: *Assange is rather ambiguous in that regard: on the one hand he argues that WikiLeaks should be seen as a storm troop that forswears the ego; on the other, it seems like an almost populist programme, considering the choice of what is publicized.*

GL: Yes, but there has also been a reversal in that regard, which took place in early 2010. Before that, celebrity status was not an issue. The question is, exactly what motivated that reversal? The obvious answer is to relate this to the decision Assange made at that time to work with regular newspapers and to cease utilizing his own organizational capacity of the Internet culture.

WvW: *In an interview, you inferred that the Internet has entered a new phase.*[13] *Through the greater use of social media, people are actually being drawn away from the open Internet, and more and more exchanges are taking place within private, controlled environments. On the other side, there is an increasing amount of control, commercialization and regulation on the open Internet. Do you believe there is a connection with the problematic of WikiLeaks here?*

13. Maurits Martijn, 'WikiLeaks moet zich niet met de inhoud bemoeien', interview with Geert Lovink, *Vrij Nederland*, 16 February 2011.

GL: Yes, a direct connection, because this touches upon the agenda of all hackers. That agenda is about openness, and currently also about the issue of net neutrality. There is a long list of militant issues. WikiLeaks is part of the hacker agenda. Its entire rhetoric comes from there, even though Assange himself has now more or less drifted in the direction of mainstream media.

WvW: *But at the same time you could also wonder, with all the databases that are being put online, what kind of emancipatory function WikiLeaks can still have for public opinion. The cables, for example, were briefly in the news; a bit of trivia was debated and a few jokes were made about world leaders. But as far as putting the topics that are hidden within them on the agenda goes, or bringing transparency to the foreign policy of the USA, publicizing them has had only a relative and mainly media effect.*

GL: I think that it has had a very big influence, and still will have. With its Cablegate, WikiLeaks has by now become a circus travelling from country to country. If you don't follow it, you wouldn't know that all sorts of things happened last month in Pakistan in which WikiLeaks was involved, and that very many things are going on in Honduras right now because of WikiLeaks. You could indeed have the impression that it is already over, yet these are things that will have consequences in the world in the long term. I see it more as a cultural change that goes much further than today's headlines.

WvW: *In any case, there is a problem with the freedom and independence of the regular media, which are censored from above, or in some instances censor themselves. Then again, you see transparency movements such as WikiLeaks that come from the tradition of hackerdom and try to find their way to openness by means of the Internet. A gap seems to be arising between vital, important information published on the Internet and the degree to which that information attracts public attention. I think that only a few people are up to date on the role of WikiLeaks in Pakistan and Honduras.*

MO: The point is that the spectacle and the banality are precisely what make it possible to break into the traditional media. I think that selective groups of informed people and networks will increasingly be better able to do something with the less visible or sensational information and spread it further – think of diplomats or journalists, for instance. What makes WikiLeaks possible, among other things because of the cables, is a database that can be referred to, accessed and studied every day. The huge volume of the leaks also makes that possible: every time a political crisis occurs, the database can be searched on the basis of a certain theme, and new things can be brought out. That won't change for a while. There are all sorts of attacks on the infrastructure of WikiLeaks, but this is a practice that can also increasingly develop at the local level. That way, outside the spectacular aspect, translations and edited versions of the leaks can end up in the mainstream media.

WvW: *WikiLeaks has anticipated situations very well by putting out certain information at precisely the right moment, so that the revelations could have their maximum effect. Can we learn something from that?*

MO: I think that the way in which the Afghanistan 'War Logs' were presented is illustrative. The press conference, how it was published in the papers . . . I don't know how all of that was prepared, but a great deal can indeed be learned from it. If only because of the incredible amount of information, which was presented in a very accessible manner. On the basis of that information, people can make projections with Google Maps, and designers can also open it up with graphics. The great challenge is to deal with that enormous data flow of information and to translate it into a digestible form that can be published in a newspaper. That way, a tipping point can be induced. WikiLeaks has done this superbly. And the whole problematic aspect of spectacle and personalization has played an important role in this.

GL: We should of course see this in the perspective of the neutralization and parallelization of the antiwar movement by the Obama administration. That's the strange thing about this medium of hactivism: it has an odd relation with the political reality of the protest movements. I don't believe in the thesis that there has been a 'virtualization or paralysation of protest', that the libidinous energy of the street is moving to the space online. The events in Egypt have shown that this is obviously not the case. But there's still the question of how these things actually do relate to one another. The relations have been lost, there is no longer any organic connection. Maybe it's because so very many processes are taking place at the same time. That makes it difficult to follow. Maybe you should determine that paralysation and politicization are occurring simultaneously, as totally contradictory movements. This would indicate that the concepts we use are no longer valid, or that in very many places there is an acceleration of processes going on that might indeed be occurring simultaneously but that are not directly related to one another.

MO: As far as protest goes, I think that the crisis actually has had a stabilizing effect on the challenging of power, and resignation is setting in. With the cutbacks, there is a reactive movement, to be sure, but the vast majority of the population thinks: 'We mustn't complain, we'll just have to tighten our belts.' You can see that there is less room for criticism. That also was demonstrated in the 1930s: the threat of a crisis incites a proclivity for authority rather than resistance.

WvW: *But couldn't it also be that, as Geert argues, different social and political processes are taking place simultaneously nowadays? That the reactions are conservative, but that this conservatism is simultaneously the germ of an unprecedentedly strong protest?*

MO: If you look at the Middle East, you see a completely different constellation than in the West. It might be connected with the global system economically, but culturally and politically it is an entirely different situation, of course. In Greece and Spain, various movements are trying to politicize the present crisis, but there is no perspective whatsoever for action. So I'm rather cynical about it. In Europe, people are again seeing that something like politics exists, that there is something like ideology. That is new, but I do not see a way out, no line of escape.

GL: The question is whether you should seek those lines of escape within the given frameworks of 'capitalistic realism', as the writer and theorist Mark Fisher describes it, for example.[14] Those frameworks are fairly hopeless. So if it has to be about a perspective of action, the question is whether to place it inside or outside that. Without becoming nationalistic, you would have to get much more into local initiatives, which are separate from the global infrastructure in which the Netherlands is so fervently participating. The dismantling of the global infrastructure: that might be a good place to start.

14. Mark Fisher, *Capitalist Realism: Is There No Alternative?* (Winchester, UK/Washington, DC: Zero Books, 2009).

This conversation took place on 29 June 2011.

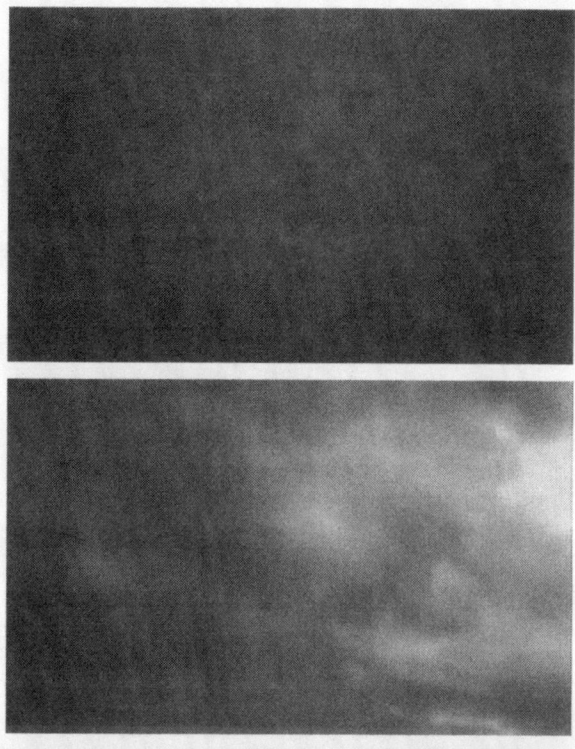

www.youtube.com/
watch?v=YrkchXCzY70

Jill Magid

Failed States

In *Failed States* Jill Magid,
who lives in Brooklyn with
her husband, Jonny, and their
son, Linus, finds a mentor in
CT, a writer and editor in
Austin, Texas with a military
and intelligence background.
A former war reporter who has
covered ten conflicts, he agrees
to train her to be an embedded
journalist with the US military
in Afghanistan. In these
excerpts Magid is confronted
with the reality of going to
war, and what is personally at
stake for her in this decision.

Failed States approaches the themes of transparency, secrecy and publicity through Magid's personal desire to engage the war on terror and its media representation through becoming an eyewitness.

The following is a series of excerpts from *Failed States*, a work-in-progress manuscript by Jill Magid.

CT travels in from Texas and visits my studio in Brooklyn to discuss a possible embed in Afghanistan.

Thursday March 4, 2010

He described what it's like going into a war zone, that it will knock you down.

You need someone there who's done it before, to warn you when you have to get down.

He crosses his arms and looks at me over his latte.

I am going with you.

That is what I wanted to hear. Hearing it changes everything.

I will be your fixer.

I don't know what that is.

A fixer is a guy who gets you in, gets you access. You could spend three weeks there just trying to figure out how the system works. I already know how the system works.

I asked him how someone does it if they don't have a fixer.

You go stay in the fanciest hotel in the area, ask the hotel manager to help you, and then give him a bribe.

So it's all about money.

Yeah. It's all about money.

As for subject matter to explore, he tells me, short of a real interrogation there is no limit.

A real interrogation is off limits, even for me as an experienced journalist with a military background.

Intelligence gathering is highly classified.

> *We could do a mock interrogation but that's a whole other ethical bag.*

I don't know what that ethical baggage is, but is anything ever at stake in a mock situation?

He gives me the soda straw analogy, based on his experience in Iraq.

> *A war zone is a very big place. Going in is like looking through a soda straw - that's how tiny your view is. Someone in another part of the war zone will have an entirely different story to tell. If you talk to the young American soldier who's training the malnourished, uneducated men that pass for Iraqi soldiers, he will tell you the war is lost. If you go to the army general who took out a host of enemy combatants earlier that day, he'll tell you it can definitely be won. And they're both right. Every story is incomplete. Afghanistan will be no different.*

After coffee, we take a walk around Williamsburg, south of Broadway. A Hasidic Jew is walking in front of us. His black hat covers his shaved head which is cast down, his eyes fixed on the ground. His black tailcoat catches in the wind. We're stretching our legs and looking for an ATM. All the Korean delis around here are owned by Hasidic Jews, but none of the Hasids shop at them.

Psychological Operations. PsyOps. This is the area he's leading me to explore. People think, because of the name, it's some kind of brainwashing or mindfuck department. I say fuck but CT doesn't. I don't think he curses, or at least he doesn't in front of me. Southern decency.

Shit. I left the electric kettle on in my studio.

> *Wars are won through perception.*

But PsyOps isn't about winning the American public over to support the war.

That's important, too. You have to protect your haunches - you don't want to get hit in the back. But, most importantly, you have to win the hearts and minds of the Iraqis or the Afghans.

CT's PsyOps contact in Iraq thinks the division should be called something else. As we walk into another deli I suggest Community Relations.

Wars today are purely psychological. They're all about changing public opinion, influencing the local population.

We're back at my studio. CT is sitting across from me at my glass desk, on the robin's egg blue chair. We still have our coats on.

My general friend in PsyOps is just a marketer. He's selling the American Dream.

CT says it with an ironic smile, like a cheesy slogan.

He's trying to convince the Iraqis that even though, yes, we just destroyed your town, we're here to help you and build you a functioning democracy. The Taliban are gone; the American system is ready to be slotted in its place. We are talking to people who read the Koran and believe that, through their system, they'll go to heaven. Can they still get to heaven through the American system? That is the essential challenge - making them believe they can.

CT will go with me to Afghanistan. He can get us through the loopholes, open the doors that would take a hell of a long time for me to pry open alone. I've never had access like this simply offered to me on a plate. He can make sure my passport goes right through. He'll make sure they don't Google me, or research my past. He can call in favors from the AP. Under normal circumstances, just getting Kevlar helmets and bulletproof vests can be difficult.

Bullets can get through the sides of the vests.

He lifts his arm up and points to just below his armpit.

You always hear the horror stories of the random bullets that slip between the ceramic chest and back plates, where the organs you need to keep safe are located.

What about my legs?

They're not protected. Neither are your arms and face.

I think about not being able to run again and then banish it from my thoughts. I feel like a false person. I don't know the reality of war. How can you from a book or a film?

The PsyOps guys are the ones who go to destroyed towns and hand out soccer balls to little boys.

A group of little Linuses. Ball was my son's first word.

Little boys love balls.

The US army prints messages on them, he explains. They're like advertisements for the US army, for the troops and for democracy.

One of the most successful PsyOps cases in Iraq involved a large truck of contraband cigarettes. The US Army stopped the truck and confiscated the cargo. The Army then stuck a sticker on each pack that said, 'If you see an IED, call this number.' It worked extraordinarily well in Baghdad. The phones rang off the hook. The locals might still see Americans as the bad guys but that doesn't mean they want their children exploding at intersections.

In Austin, Texas. CT and I are driving to borrow guns to
use during my Hostile Environment Training — one-on-one
instruction for my embed with the US Military in Afghanistan

Saturday June 5, 2010

We drive to his friend's place to borrow guns. We pull up
to the small house of a guy in a Texas T-shirt with a weird
mouth (some type of birth defect, I think). He lives there
with his wife who is storing her dad's guns. Once an avid
gun collector, her father's now a sad lonely man who lives in
Mexico with the women he pays for because it's cheap. In the
car after we leave, CT and I discuss how there's something
indescribably sad about a 60-year-old single man pretending
to live the life of a playboy. Mouth guy's wife works for a
senator at the capitol. Some months ago, a young man drew
and fired a gun on the south steps of the capitol building
— an incident I, weirdly enough, witnessed. She's taking a
concealed handgun course. Everyone in the office was advised
to do so.

She has two guns to lend us, both cop guns with string ties
around them so they can't be fired accidentally. Her father
prepared them for her — carefully, like this — when he
left for Mexico, even though she did not want them. They
make her nervous — she has a child in the house. CT is
impressed by how safely the guns are kept. We will borrow
them for shooting practice at the ranch tomorrow. He casually
mentions as we step off their front porch that, at some point
tomorrow, he is going to abduct me. He just slips that in.

It will be a three-hour process, he tells me. And even
though I know it's going to happen, I will have an emotional
reaction.

It seems very late when we get back to his house.

The one thing about being married is that I cannot sleep alone,
he tells me as we say goodnight. It doesn't sound like an
invitation. He is upstairs alone and I am down here awake

and alone and Linus feels so far away. Jonny doesn't. I feel Jonny. If Jonny knew exactly what we were up to here — shooting guns, learning how to treat a sucking chest wound, prepping for an abduction — he'd wonder why I am even doing this. Sometimes I wonder the same. Is this where my work with the Dutch secret service left me? I think I preferred the distance.

CT's house in Texas.

Sunday June 6, 2010

We sit at the table in the living room.

Abduction and Interrogation. Rule one: Try not to get abducted.

I laugh. He doesn't.

Unit cohesion and unit Integrity. It's a romantic idea. Stay together, don't leave dead bodies on the battleground. Only four people have gone missing in Afghanistan and Iraq combined. That's how seriously this rule is taken. Well armed, large units; always at least two vehicles in a convoy; always an even number of people.

Sometimes, though, ambushes are complex.

That's when they come at you from more than one place.

He arranges the objects on the table to demonstrate: A large fold in the tablecloth is a mountain ridge, a wide book is the road, a smaller book the convoy.

The IED detonates with the first vehicle but then there's a boom on either side and suddenly the convoy is boxed in, people are shooting from the mountain ridge. You fear this. Am I entering a kill zone? No matter how well you prepare, you just can't rule out the possibility of a complex ambush. There are always possible kill zones. Try to be ready.

Situational Awareness is sometimes referred to as SA or Sierra Alpha.

I'm going to teach you the military alphabet.

My homework is to learn the phonetic alphabet.

Do you know what Whisky Tango Foxtrot means? What the fuck. You'll hear that a lot.

So what you do is get everyone together and drive the hell out of the kill zone. Don't stop. Flank: try to maneuver through and push past. Always turn around and fight - never just flee. If one of the vehicles is dead, you have the dangerous job of transferring the stranded soldiers into an active one. That switch is a highly vulnerable move. That's when bad things can happen. The insurgents want to grab you, or capture the vehicle with you inside of it.

I think the first option sounds worse.

They know the power of a US hostage. Danny Pearl was a huge success for Al-Qaeda. Jill Carroll, too. 'I don't want to be in a beheading video.' 'I don't want to be seen in an orange jumpsuit.' You'll hear the guys say that a lot.

I imagine Jonny and Linus and feel like I'm going to vomit. And then I remember this really fucked up scene in a movie that was, perversely, extremely sexy. What movie was that? I saw it on TV, on a good cable channel, like IFC or something. A woman is being held hostage. The man who brings her food doesn't speak her language but an attraction grows. She's kept tied by her hands to a wooden ceiling rafter, standing on a white bed, a beautiful old one with white sheets and a matching white bedspread. He comes in and puts down her tray of food. I'm not sure how she's supposed to eat since she's tied up like that or if he's meant to spoon-feed her or what, but he lifts her skirt — she's naked underneath — and goes down on her until she comes. He leaves the room straight after, no words are spoken. I can't recall if he left the tray on the bed or if he put it on the floor or if it just disappeared during a jump cut.

I ask CT if he's ever seen one of those beheading videos. He calls them snuff tapes. He's watched them when he's been required to for a story. He doesn't like to watch violent Hollywood movies.

No gore, he says. Horror movies like that are real.

I have always known that.

CT's personal wish is never to be a hostage.

Don't bite, kick, or fight. They will kill you immediately. Some men want that, just to be killed right there, to avoid the orange jumpsuit and the horror their families will endure. So they bite and kick. It's suicide.

I ask why the snuff tape is created in the first place.

It's a terror tool, he says. The image strikes fear, demoralizes the enemy, sows the seed of low morale back home.

As a journalist he is obliged to report on other journalists killed by insurgents.

Those are important stories. But the challenge is how to do so without furthering the enemy's goal. Does the video need to be seen by the public or can it be communicated with words alone? Words are powerful but the image is a hundredfold more.

I feared this. I've always wanted words to be just as powerful. I want my words to be powerful.

You have to get the news across without doing the enemy's propagandist work for them. The US military produces official US army videos shot from Apache helicopters. The other side releases videos showing US soldiers being killed by Juba snipers. To counter this, the US releases gun camera videos. It's tit for tat.

CT chooses to describe videos rather than redistributing them.

It's not smart to resist if you are taken hostage. The longer you survive, the better your chances of getting out. A hostage scenario is a mental game of wits. 85 percent of survival is mental.

I ask him if he feels invincible after seeing so much, and he says, *No, the opposite has happened. I realize my fragility and how human I am.*

I don't believe him.

You have to have a strategy for being abducted. The first stage, the shock of capture, is predictable. Resistance is pointless. Bite and kick and you're pretty much committing suicide. If you're too much work they will simply shoot you. Or you could have the worst of both worlds, where they beat you up and keep you without medical treatment. But you'll be roughed up no matter what. If you're captured in a group they'll pick out whoever seems to be the leader and make an example of him. Fade in and be colorless. Go limp, become grey. The other guy they kill is the one who has a complete breakdown, because that guy's annoying.

You are not a leader, you obey and cooperate. They are assessing you. They will take your press card and passport and look you up. Say yes, say no, don't expand. Remember, their adrenalin is pumping. They are scared, too.

Next comes the interrogation phase. You tell them, I am not a combatant. I have no obligation to the military, no obligation to keep secrets. I am a mother.

Your main strategy, if you are kidnapped, is being a mom. Having Linus and Jonny. They will want to know about your family. If you're not a journalist, not a spy, what are you? Why are you here without your husband? You're going to have to lie about your name. They might have the resources to Google you. Be prepared to lie about being Jewish. If they ask about your name, Magid - what type of name is Magid?

It's Jewish.

No. It's Lebanese Christian.

I guess I'd better start researching what it is to be Lebanese.

No no no. He waves away my words. *They don't know shit about Lebanese Christianity. What does Majid mean in Arabic? It's probably the same in Hebrew. Look it up.*

(I just looked it up as I type. It means 'glorious' in Arabic. In Hebrew, which I know, it means 'itinerant storyteller.' I love that, but glorious isn't bad, either).

Look it up because I'm sure it's a common word in both languages. As a journalist you have to make up your story and know it. You don't want a complicated story.

He makes one up for me.

OK, so your family left Lebanon in the early 1900s. Don't even mention the word Jewish - do not plant ideas! You're not even remotely Jewish so not a thought in your head about it. You're fourth generation American. Anything factual - volunteer it. And tell as few lies as possible. Physical abuse is most likely if you're impatient or if they know you're lying. Always maintain eye contact when you're lying. If you look down or to the left, they'll know. Whenever you have to tell a lie, take a breath and look straight into their eyes. Don't blink.

Tell them whatever you know about the army to show them you're not useful. Let everything out because you don't know anything important.

Jesus. If that isn't humbling.

You're not hurting anyone. Your knowledge isn't deep enough.

What, I wonder, if I want it to be?

You'll have the same interrogator for the long term. He will establish himself as your alpha male.

I think he actually said your alpha leader, but I imagine him to be male.

Remember you are powerless - including over your future. This is what they want you to think.

If you were the enemy and this was a US interrogation, you'd be stripped naked. Clothing is emotional armor. It provides psychological protection. Being stripped works on everyone but especially Muslims, for whom it carries added insult. Your captors will control your whole environment: your room temperature, your food, your sleep. The interrogator manipulates everything so that you'll submit. Adding physical pain only damages the process. The interrogator does not want you to emotionally collapse. You don't want people to shut down on you, like a rose folding in on itself, back into a bud - excuse the metaphor.

I think for CT referencing roses feels emasculating.

It's like this.

He folds his arms, locking his elbows across his torso, and hollows his chest, his head dropping forward and his chin hitting his collarbone.

If you reach this point they'll know you've mentally disengaged, that you can't answer any more questions. Take

*the slaps on the face when they come. They will. Hardly
react to them. But don't do this too early otherwise
they'll know you're faking. Wait at least eight hours.*

Eight hours?

*A bad interrogator might still try to torture you even
then. Hope for a good one. And foremost in your mind: I
will survive. I will walk out of here back to Linus.*

There is something dirty about him using Linus's name. It's
just a word to him, completely detached from the boy Linus
who is also — secondly — my son. To CT he is an anchor,
an escape tool for me from a bad situation. Linus is only
language in his mouth, coming out as strategy, and somehow it
spoils the boy to whom it is attached and I feel gross that I
let it happen.

Back in Brooklyn, a few nights after I'd returned from my
training, I asked Jonny if he felt his life was his own. No,
he said, he did not, almost before I'd even got the question
out.

Did that change when you got together with me or after Linus
was born?

Linus - he pauses - *and maybe a little with you*. He thinks
some more. *I don't express myself so much anymore*. He is
thoughtful. *But I do express myself through Linus*.

That's interesting. You interpret the question of whether
your life is your own in terms of self-expression?

He looks at me, confused, so I continue. I was thinking about
how everyone always warns you when you have a kid that your
life won't be your own anymore because you're responsible for
another person's. The purpose of your life becomes to serve
the needs of your child.

Oh, well yes, that is also part of it. That is also true.

He breaks eye contact with me and is quiet for a moment.
That's depressing. He looks back.

*But your life is always your own. Your life is always
yours. Who else's could it be?*

Zachary Formwalt

Selections from an Archive of Images of Economy

The Amsterdam-based artist Zachary Formwalt investigates whether it is possible to make capital visible as part of the economy. The idea is not to unveil, but to give the abstract notion of capital a visible form and turn it into an object

See: www.zacharyformwalt.com

In this contribution he presents selections from an archive of images of economy begun in earnest in mid-2006, as an attempt to understand the mechanisms used to relate photographs to economic events. The archive was ended in disinterest at some point in 2008, as the crisis wore on and the relation of photographs to economic 'performance' itself became a subject of interest in the media.

The images on the last spread come from the following newspapers on the dates given:

2007

28.07
The Guardian

16.08
The Guardian,
Tagesspiegel

17.08
Berliner Zeitung,
Tagesspiegel,
Handelsblatt,
Financial Times

18.08
Tagesspiegel,
The Guardian

20.08
Süddeutsche Zeitung

25.08
Financial Times

13.12
The Guardian

2008

05.01
The Guardian

19.01
The Guardian

22.01
Het Parool,
AD,
NRC Handelsblad

26.01
International
Herald Tribune

19.03
Aftenposten,
International
Herald Tribune,
Financial Times

27.03
Financial Times

12.07
The Guardian

20.09
The Guardian

30.09
metro (Amsterdam),
The Guardian

01.10
metro (Amsterdam),
Financial Times

07.10
The Times,
Financial Times,

11.10
Financial Times,
The Guardian,
International
Herald Tribune

14.10
de Volkskrant

Sven Lütticken

Secrets of the See-Through Factory

On Intervening in Opaque Transparency

Art historian and critic Sven Lütticken sketches how concepts such as transparency and opacity, openness and secrecy are being used by artists in increasingly subtle ways. They are particularly interested in the question of how we can make ourselves 'visible as something other (either more or less) than the kind of subject to which we tend to be reduced'.

We live in the age of open secrets. More than anything else, WikiLeaks has shown the relative weakness, in today's global empire, of the essential Enlightenment act that is the revealing of hidden secrets. Such revelations may endanger American or European troops in Afghanistan, but in Europe and the USA their effects seem limited, as there is plenty of online outrage, but little in the way of political effects – and WikiLeaks has itself come under attack for its 'lack of transparency'. Perhaps it is one of the 'zones of opacity' that the Invisible Committee deems necessary.[1] According to this logic, a prying police state that wants to turn its subjects into see-through citizens has to be countered with opacity even while the state's own zones of opacity are relentlessly critiqued. After all, is this 'transparent', 'democratic' system not a de facto conspiracy in the service of the happy few? But the strategies of radical groups and their corporate antagonists mirror each other: Julian Assange approved of the *News of the World* hacking people's phones, even while bemoaning that these practices did not go far enough.[2] He did not pause to question the complete perversion of the ideology of transparency in the hands of Rupert Murdoch and his goons.

1. Comité Invisible, *L'Insurrection qui vient* (Paris: La Fabrique, 2007), 97.

2. See this interview from 2009: http://barefootintocyberspace.com/2011/07/27/assange_transcript/

It is a recurring feature of modernity that attacks on an opaque system that functions as a de facto conspiracy themselves take on a conspiratorial character – from the Enlightenment (Masonic lodges) via anarchist cells and Georges Bataille's Acéphale and various groups of the 1970s to, precisely, the Invisible Committee and WikiLeaks.[3] Such oppositional forces produce strange blends of opacity and transparency – *opaque transparency* and *transparent opacity* – that mirror the state of affairs they oppose. Thus rather than with a static opposition between hiding and uncovering, we are dealing with a dazzling dialectic. More than ever, it is futile to side with either opacity or transparency as such. Rather than turning openness into a cult or promoting the cult of secrecy for its own sake, the aim should be to examine the collusion between the two poles so as to develop strategies for prying open the cracks in the apparently seamless surface of opaque transparency – to exacerbate the latent contradictions and turn them into overt antinomies.

3. On the late eighteenth and early nineteenth centuries, see J.M. Roberts, *The Mythology of the Secret Societies* (London: Watkins, 2008). See also the essays 'Secret Publicity' and 'The conspiracy of Publicness' in Sven Lütticken, *Secret Publicity: Essays on Contemporary Art*, (Rotterdam: NAi Publishers, 2006).

This is where art comes in. Not only have various artistic and quasi-artistic groups, from symbolism to the Situationist International via surrealism and Bataille, taken on cult-like or conspiratorial forms, but the very fabric of the modern work of art is an object lesson in the dialectic of opacity and transparency. For much of modernity, visual art has perfected techniques for mystifying through openness, laying bare its procedures with obscure results. The work of art being a commodity that is both eccentric and exemplary, art can be seen as a form of political economy that *intervenes in* as much as it reflects on Art today's opaquely transparent and transparently opaque spectacle.[4]

4. My earlier formulation of art as a 'mute form of political economy' does not imply that art is doomed only to reflect impotently, which is how Nikos Papastergiadis seems to take it in 'Aesthetics and Politics in the Age of Ambient Spectacles' (*Contemporary Art and Culture Broadsheet* 39, no. 1 (2010), 33-39). It is mute in so far as it falls short of all discursive conventions and of academic standards; this is also its potential strength. It is a form of praxis that can intervene in and rearticulate the regime of the (in)visible. At the same time, I remain doggedly convinced that one needs to go beyond grandiloquent claims for the potentiality of aesthetic practice, and confront the antinomies that both enable and – at times – cripple it.

Structure and System

Theodor W. Adorno analysed the development of modern art in terms of an ever more rational construction.[5] However, this constructive rationality did not result in works that were transparent and devoid of mystery. On the contrary, it is the apparent rationality of ever more carefully planned construction that cements their status as riddles.[6] In a disenchanted world dominated by technocratic 'purposive rationality', Adorno averred that art constitutes a scandal because it cannot rid itself of magic, of primeval enchantment. Even the most constructive modern art remains fundamentally mimetic. In its mimicking of rational construction methods it is a kind of 'secularized magic' that reveals itself as make-believe, as *Schein,* as illusive appearance.[7]

5. Theodor W. Adorno, *Ästhetische Theorie* (Frankfurt am Main: Suhrkamp, 1970), 90-91.

6. Ibid., 182.

7. Ibid., 86-87.

Some modern artists went very far in their mimetic appropriation of technocratic rationality. This is true in particular of some movements in European art around the 1960s, including Zero in Germany and the Dutch Nul group. A fetish in these circles was the notion of structure, praised by Jan Schoonhoven in terms that barely disguise their Platonism: 'Structure gives line and form substance. Structure is reality. Structure determines the effects of light.'[8] Structural transparency also suggested a social analogy: transparent, non-hierarchical art for a modern and rational society.[9] This analogy broke down in the late 1960s, with Sol LeWitt's emphasis on the *irrational* nature of grid structures, and with Hans Haacke's investigation of (social) systems.

8. A 1959 statement by Schoonhoven quoted in Janneke Wesseling, *Alles was mooi: een geschiedenis van de Nul-beweging* (Amsterdam: Meulenhoff/Landshoff, 1989), 53.

Haacke had actually operated in the margins of the ZERO movement, collaborating for instance on the aborted 'Zero op zee' event that the Dutch Nul group attempted to

9. '*Geen hiërarchie, we kozen voor ordening, heel objectief.*' ('No hierarchy: we opted for arrangement, very objectively.') Schoonhoven, from a 1979 interview, quoted in: Ibid., 50.

organize by the sea in Scheveningen. Haacke created pieces that often used modern materials to investigate natural phenomena – his *Condensation Cubes* were closed Plexiglas cubes that are more or less transparent depending on the room temperature and the resulting amount of condensation inside the cube. For the critic Jack Burnham, Haacke's practice was one important indicator of a changing relationship between art and technology, as well as of a move away from object-based art to *systems art*. According to Burnham, the structures of most 1950s and early 1960s art remained ultimately illusory, belonging to the world of appearances: they were still visual compositions rather than functional constructions.[10] But more fundamentally, the analysis had to move up a level, from structure to system. Systems theory, with its roots in biology, promised to be a new paradigm that would in fact 'diminish the distinction between biological and non-biological systems', and a new systems-oriented art would 'deal less with artifacts contrived for their formal value, and increasingly with men enmeshed *with* and *within* purposeful responsive systems'.[11]

10. 'Though a high correlation between visual and structural logic may exist in engineering, surprisingly little attempt has been made to establish such a logic in sculpture – and when an attempt has been made, it has usually been a pseudo-attempt, rather than one which is strictly consistent with the properties of the materials. Engineering in sculpture – with very few exceptions – has been a matter of visual assimilation, not function.' Jack Burnham, *Beyond Modern Sculpture: The Effects of Science and Technology on the Sculpture of This Century* (New York: George Braziller, 1968), 155.

11. Ibid., 363.

In the late 1960s, Haacke moved from investigating 'natural systems' (as in his pieces dealing with wind or condensation) to 'social systems'.[12] Haacke started presenting visitor polls as works of art in 1969 with his *Gallery-Goers' Birthplace and Residence* profile at the Howard Wise Gallery, the viewers becoming cybernetic performers by answering questions. Polls and profiles would go on to become ever more prominent in the economy, up to today's online profiles. Neither a technocratic affirmation nor an abstract rejection, Haacke's pieces attempt to play the system, to intervene in it through strategic mimicry.

12. See also Marga Bijvoet, *Art as Inquiry*, Part II, Chapter 4, http://www.stichting-mai.de/hwg/amb/aai/art_as_inquiry_05.htm.

In the 1970 'Information' show at New York's Museum of Modern Art, which was shaped by cybernetics, Haacke presented a poll with one political question, on New York Governor Nelson Rockefeller's stance on Vietnam. That Rockefeller was also a MoMA trustee was not stated, but for those in the know it served to underscore the interrelations between the art world and other social systems.[13] For Burnham's 'Software' show at the Jewish Museum, also in 1970, Haacke planned a computer version of the visitor poll, allowing for a more complex series of questions that he developed in the form of flow chart diagrams. Due to technical difficulties, this version was

13. Julia Bryan-Wilson, *Art Workers: Radical Practice in the Vietnam Era* (Berkeley/Los Angeles: University of California Press, 2009), 190-193.

not realized.[14] Haacke's surviving flow charts, with their mixture of personal and general political questions, are not so much about making 'the system' transparent as they are about our implication in it, and the effect of our specific situations on our perceptions and preconceptions.

14. 'According to my memory, the people from MIT who were meant to do the computer programming for it were either overextended due to their work on other projects in the show or were not able to do it.' Quote from an email by Hans Haacke, 28 April 2011.

In systems theory, 'the system' risks becoming a theoretical fetish, a quasi-divine entity that governs fish and humans alike. But in Haacke's work the emphasis is not on system-theoretical analysis so much as it is on *intervention* in systems. His *Visitors' Profiles* and other pieces constitute interventions in social systems that *make visible their peculiar dialectic of opacity and transparency.* Opinion polls were regularly presented as typifying an 'open society' in which the citizen-consumer was 'king'; on the other hand, certain sociologists presented such instruments (with some justification) as just another tool in the arsenal of the 'hidden persuaders'. Rather than either condemning or praising the opinion poll, Haacke puts it to use, subverts it – asking questions about Nelson Rockefeller in a white cube. Haacke's work makes things visible, but at the same time it does not presume that making things visible is enough; gestures have to be timed and located very precisely – as with his *Manet-PROJEKT '74* in Cologne.[15]

15. *Manet-PROJEKT '74* consists of a series of panels investigating the provenance of Manet's asparagus still-life from the collection of the Wallraf-Richartz-Museum in Cologne, as well as the Nazi past of Hermann Josef Abs, a banker who was the then chairman of the museum's board. Made for the exhibition Project '74, the piece was twice censored: when Haacke was not allowed to show his work, Daniel Buren integrated copies of Haacke's panels into his own project. They were quickly pasted over on behest of the museum director.

This is embedded, tactical critique that one could describe – in cybernetic terms – as mutated and unwanted feedback. If the gesture is too massive or too abstract, the effect is questionable. Whether 'revelations' of 'hidden secrets' as such are effective is highly doubtful. A few years before WikiLeaks went stratospheric, Walid Raad already addressed the limits of openness in a lecture/performance in which he traced covert CIA rendition flights and the people and (sham) companies enabling them. As dotted lines appeared gradually on the projection screen, Raad quoted the mocking questions a friend had asked him: 'Is there anything more fashionable anymore than to make public the contradictions at the heart of the US administration's war on terror? ... What if these policies are effective NOT because they have not been examined enough? What if these policies are effective NOT because no one has bothered to show that they are short-sighted and ill-conceived? What if those who kidnap and torture today depend on public exposure and visibility as part and parcel of what they do? In other words, what if these things can go on today because they are too clearly visible, broad-

Hans Haacke, flow chart (one of four sheets) for unrealized version of *Visitors' Profile* conceived for Jack Burnham's *Software* (1970).

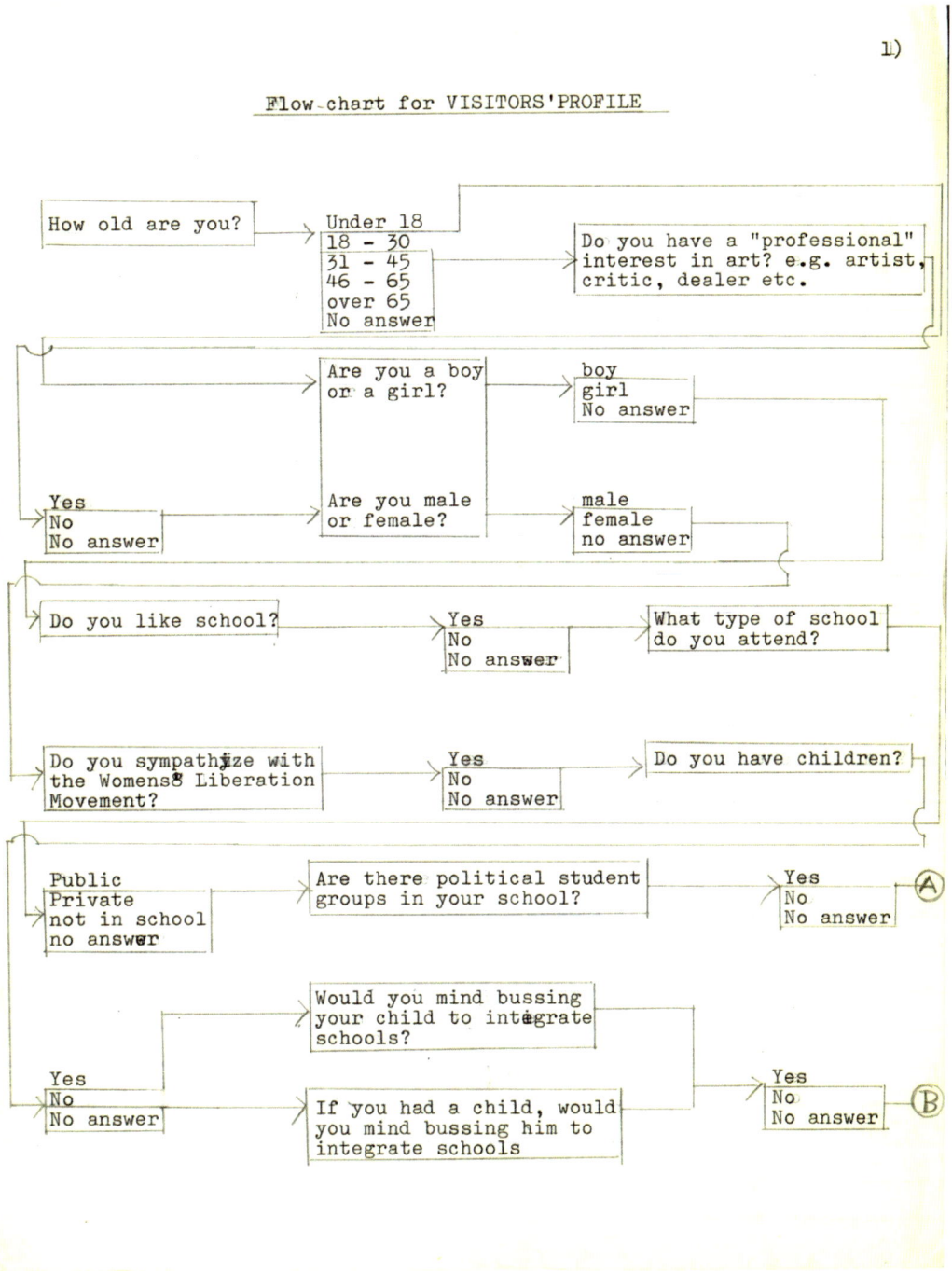

Flow-chart for VISITORS'PROFILE

Hans Haacke, flow chart (two of four sheets) for unrealized version of *Visitors' Profile* conceived for Jack Burnham's *Software* (1970).

2)

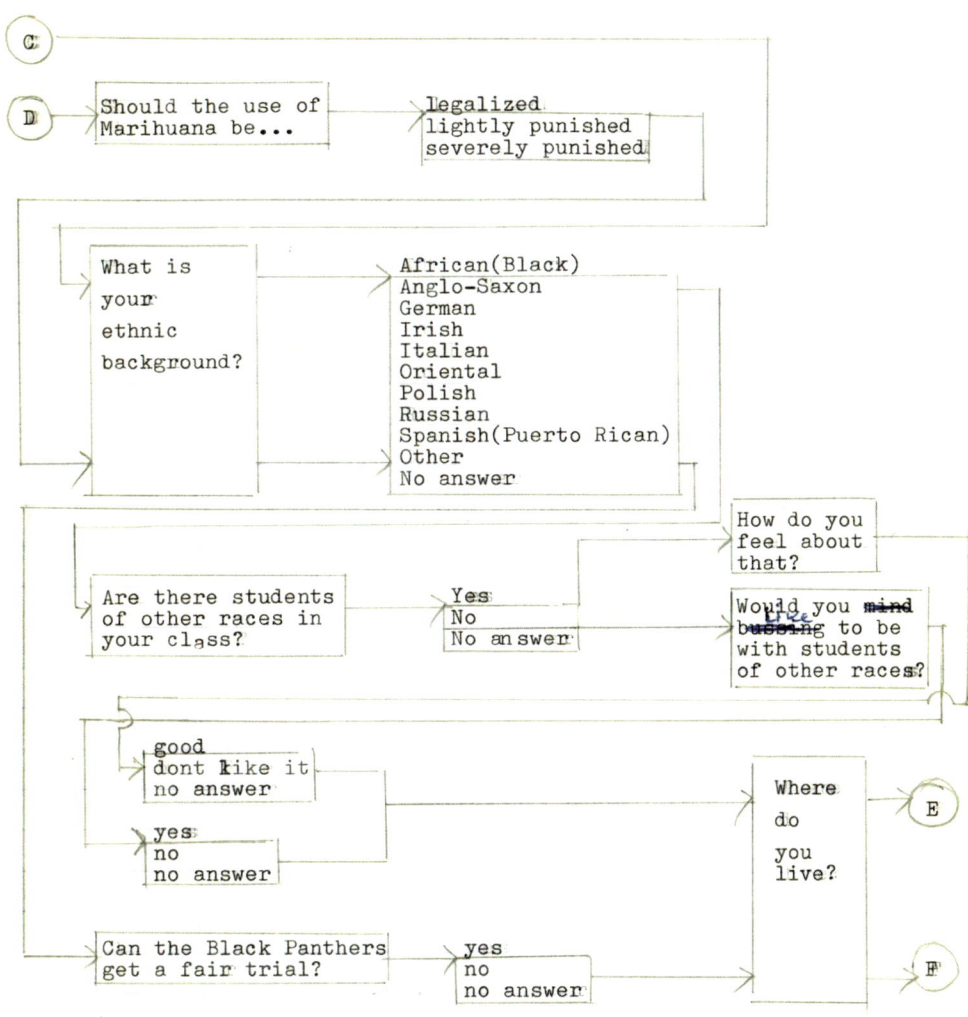

C

D

Should the use of
Marihuana be...

legalized
lightly punished
severely punished

What is
your
ethnic
background?

African(Black)
Anglo-Saxon
German
Irish
Italian
Oriental
Polish
Russian
Spanish(Puerto Rican)
Other
No answer

How do you
feel about
that?

Are there students
of other races in
your class?

Yes
No
No answer

Would you mind
like
bussing to be
with students
of other races?

good
dont like it
no answer

yes
no
no answer

Where
do
you
live?

E

Can the Black Panthers
get a fair trial?

yes
no
no answer

F

Secrets of the See-Through Factory

cast live, entirely predictable – in fact, they have been announced outright in advance?'[16]

16. Walid Raad, 'I Feel a Great Desire to Meet the Masses Once Again (Part 1)', typescript, 2007.

Object and Thing

The issue of the (im)mobility of persons in turn has its counterparts among objects. In works from 2003 to 2005 such as the film *Casio, Seiko, Sheraton, Toyota, Mars,* the photo archive *Untitled (Archive Iraq)* and the photo/text piece *The Site,* Sean Snyder has charted trajectories of a different nature than Raad's CIA flights, though these trajectories are equally part and parcel of the 'War on Terror' – which in Snyder's work becomes a series of appearances of Casio watches, Toyotas, Coke cans and Mars bars in the war theatre of the Middle East. Here the War on Terror is not about any great ideals but about access to and the deployment of commodities – products that in Snyder's work serve as symptomatic indicators of the real interests at stake. However, their visibility is in turn oddly opaque, and they seem to be playing games with us – like the whimsical Mars bars and Spam cans that appear to move around in various images and descriptions of Saddam Hussein's underground hideout. Is their presence just another convenient 'public exposure'?

Snyder shows snapshots from the social life of objects. In this, the work can be seen as a rejoinder to the commodity art of the late 1980s, when pieces by artists such as Haim Steinbach glorified commodity fetishism as the play of coded difference. 'Desire' and 'code' were the *mots du jour*, and the work's coded differences resulted in a curiously opaque transparency. The formal play is enjoyable, while the suggestion that it is all that matters is somewhat unsettling. The simple structures of the triangular shelves with their evenly spaced commodities no longer claim to be exercises in 'rational construction', nor do they critique such claims. They celebrate their shiny opacity, their literally superficial qualities. What matters is surface; the object becomes a projection screen. In spite of or because of his works' complicity in a highly destructive economy, Steinbach thus articulated a very real characteristic of the Reagan era. Precisely in going implementing the passion for the code, so rigorously, the works retain an oddly resistant quality.[17]

But what about the invisible obverse of these commodities' alluring surfaces? The practice inaugurated by artist Kobe Matthys in 1992 under the generic name of Agency paralleled Snyder's in that it took a decisive step beyond commodity art – in the process

17. In the late 1980s and early 1990s, Haacke made a number of small works mocking Appropration Art and its take on the Duchampian ready-made. Particularly interesting is *Baudrichard's Ecstasy* (1988), consisting of an ironing board with a bucket and a gilded urinal through which water is pumped to and from the bucket – a closed system.

Walid Raad, illustrations used during the lecture/performance
'I Feel a Great Desire to Meet the Masses Once Again', in which
he traced secret cia flights.

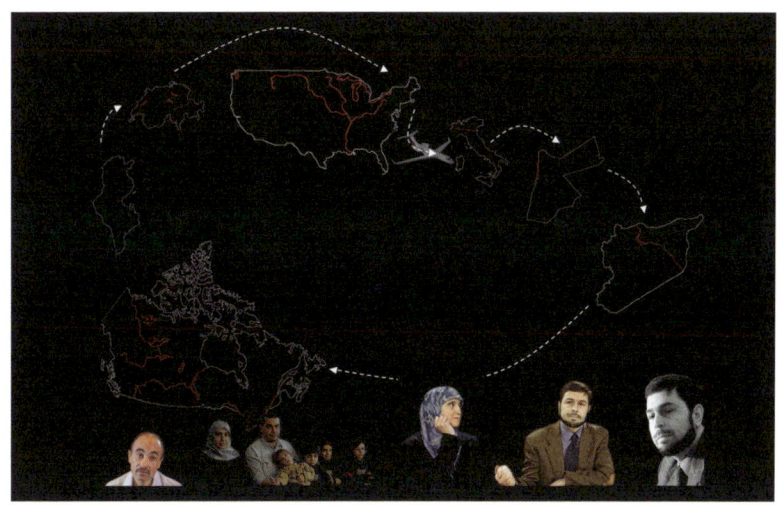

reactivating aspects of the art of the late 1960s and early 1970s, such as Conceptual Art's focus on protocols and contracts. Agency collects 'Things' whose status has been contested in lawsuits over intellectual property rights; it 'convenes' these Things in the form of 'assemblies' (exhibitions or events) that allow for an investigation of these cases. Agency's Things range from a TV recording of a trained elephant to computer-generated bingo numbers, an 'Uncle Sam' bank, children's costumes and various books, records and films. In all these cases, the main question is whether we are dealing with 'original works' that can be copyrighted, raising questions on subjecthood and authorship. Can a trained elephant's behaviour be copyrighted by its trainer? Can a book said to have been dictated by spirits to a medium be subject to copyright? Can computer-generated bingo numbers?

Two of Agency's Things are based on the famous magic trick of *The Woman Sawn in Half*, which Horace Goldin sought to protect both in copyright law and in patent law in the early 1920s.[18] When a film company released a short subject purporting to show how the trick was done, Goldin sued, and lost (*Thing 000809*). Much later, in the 1930s, he sued again when Camel Cigarettes published an ad in their series 'It's fun to be fooled . . . It's more fun to know', which also purported to reveal the truth (*Thing 000842*). He lost again, in part because of his own patent, which qualified as public information: at least in theory, the secret was already out. What is interesting about these Things in particular is that they almost seem to allegorize the commodity and its magical promise of shiny and eternal newness – which we know full well hides programmed obsolescence. The lady sawn in half and reconstituted is the hollow promise of any product: the reversal of entropy.

The notion of the *thing* is prominent in contemporary theory, and one might say that the thing has emerged as something that is *both more and less than an object*. In W.J.T. Mitchell's words: '"Things" are no longer passively waiting for a concept, theory, or sovereign subject to arrange them in ordered ranks of objecthood. "The Thing" rears its head – a rough beast or sci-fi monster, a repressed returnee, an obdurate materiality, a stumbling block, and an object lesson.'[19] Rather than building a wall between art and thingness, the work of art should be analysed as just such a sci-fi monster – a monster that itself has a secondary *agency*, as the anthropologist Alfred Gell has argued.[20] While objects are named and categorized, part of a system of objects, thingness is resistant to such ordered objecthood. If we grant

18. These Things were 'called forth' by Kobe Matthys on 24 June 2010 at Casco, Office for Art, Design and Theory, in Utrecht.

19. W. J. T. Mitchell, *What Do Pictures Want? The Lives and Loves of Images* (Chicago and London: University of Chicago Press, 2005), 112.

20. Alfred Gell, *Art and Agency: An Anthropological Theory* (Oxford: Oxford University Press, 2008).

Sean Snyder, *The Site*, 2004-2005, Lightjet prints on paper, mounted on foam board and text panels.
Courtesy the artist and Lisson Gallery

Sean Snyder, *Untitled, (Archive Iraq)*, 2003-2005, Lightjet prints on aluminium.

Sean Snyder, *Untitled, (Archive Iraq)*, 2003-2005, Lightjet prints on aluminium.

that *works of art are both more and less than other types of things,* this should be regarded not as an incentive to exacerbate and fetishize those differences, but rather as a point of departure for examining the complex inter-relationships between various kinds of things, and the ways in which certain works of art problematize and transform this very rela-tionship. The Marxian theory of commodity fetishism has long drawn attention to the 'theological whims' of commodities; these seeming social relationships between things are ultimately seen as distorted reflections of relationships between people. However, do the commodities in turn not play an active role in inflecting and shaping human relations?[21]

21. See also Joshua Simon, 'Neo-Materialism, Part One: The Com-modity and the Exhibition', in *e-flux journal* no. 20 (November 2010), http://www.e-flux.com/journal/view/182: 'Marx's quote above seems to suggest that *we* are actually a mate-rialization of *their* relations. Consider our bodies – blood sugar levels, kid-ney stones, cholesterol levels, or can-cerous pollution. In our relations with commodities, we no longer have the ability to decide between production or consumption, improvisation or function, profit or loss. It is in this way that, as part of the social relations that materialize within it, the com-modity gains a life of its own – beyond even the means of its inven-tion: design, manufacturing, production, marketing, shipment, dis-posal, and evacuation.'

Hito Steyerl's recent film *In Free Fall* (2010) focuses on the 'lives' of Boeing airplanes that vegetate on a junkyard in the Mojave Desert, investigating their biographies from Howard Hughes and the Israeli air force to being recycled as DVDs. Depending on market fluctuations, planes may be used for movie productions or be sold to China for their scrap metal. *In Free Fall* does not fetishize the social relations between things. Both object and subject – or thing and person – act and are acted upon in a bewilderingly complex political economy. Steyerl's camera-man, for instance, lost a significant amount of work in Hollywood because of the crash of the DVD market due to online streaming and file sharing. While it might seem that with *In Free Fall*, Steyerl 'has turned from the essayistic subject to the essayistic object', it may be more pre-cise to say that the film focuses on objects as having a certain derivative and secondary *agency* that affects lives.[22] It is by making such connec-tions that Steyerl's film intervenes in an eco-nomic system that instrumentalizes transpar-ency and opacity, openness and secrecy, with equal ease.

22. Kerstin Stakemeier, 'Plane Destructive: The Recent Films of Hito Steyerl', http://www.metamute.org/en/articles/plane_destructive_the_recent_films_of_hito_steyerl.

(In)Visibility and the Sub-Subject

Visibility does not equal transparency: complete transparency, after all, would pose no obstacle to light and hence produce no image. One might say that any image is the product of a particular admixture of opacity and transparency. Images have a tendency to be used as allegor-ical emblems, and this is particularly true of images of (relative) transparency. Think of Berlin's renovated Reichstag building, which now houses the Bundestag: while the use of mirrors and glass in de plenary chamber under the central dome can be somewhat dizzying, the bright space is usually presented as embodying an open and transparent democracy. Think of Volkswagen's 'Transparent Factory' in Dresden, in which we are shown how cars are assembled by robots, as if by magic, while we do not get to see the actual production of the individual parts and the financial and political wheeling and dealing.

As artist Zachary Formwalt notes in his book *Reading the Economist* (2010) on the basis of Marx's notations on *The Economist*: 'The invisibility of the instruments of exchange was the measure of their efficiency; the less visible, the more efficient they were in the circulation of capital.'[23] Formwalt's video film *In Place of Capital* (2009) muses on the (un)representability of capital in relation to the invention of photography, and in particular Fox Talbot's photographs of the London

23. Zachary Formwalt, *Reading the Economist* (Utrecht/Porto: Casco/Serralves, 2010), 16.

Stock Exchange, in which passers-by appear as immaterial spectres due to long camera exposures. *Reading the Economist* is a similar montage inquiry into capital and visibility. When a crisis hits, 'suddenly visible instruments of exchange are all that will do and the sudden demand for such instruments, for all other instruments to be converted into cash, or something very close to it, produces a rupture in the field of visibility – the financial suddenly appears directly, not as something buried comfortably behind anonymous glass building facades or company logos in the Business and Finance sections of the press, but directly on the front pages as people demanding their money . . .'[24]   24. Ibid., 135.

Such scenes, such symptomatic 'assemblies', show abstract capital taking on visible form, congealing into thingness. This is not some abstract gesture of revelation, but a symptomatic manifestation of tensions within the system, which takes the form of specific constellations – improvised structures – emerging in the visual plane. If, in this case, this is the result of unplanned collective action (a kind of swarm-like activity), there are also possibilities for more strategic interventions that upset the dominant regime of (in)visibility, its particular collusion of opacity and transparency. Again, such interventions have to be precise and begin at home, so to speak. They have to show our implication in something that is more concrete than a/the system – in social structures or networks that implicate us. How do we intervene in such sub-systemic constellations in ways that make us visible as something other (either more or less) than the kind of subject to which we tend to be reduced?

In 2011, a number of artists announced a boycott of the Guggenheim

Volkswagen's so-called 'Transparent Factory' ('Gläserne Manufaktur') in Dresden.

Zachary Formwalt, stills from *In the Place of Capital*, 2009.
HD-video, 24.30 min.

Museum if the abysmal treatment of workers on the construction site of the Guggenheim Abu Dhabi – the latest outlet of the McGuggenheim franchise – continued. Walid Raad was one of the boycott's initiators, and Hans Haacke supported the campaign.[25] Guggenheims in New York, in Bilbao, in Abu Dhabi: a system of architectural objects serving the circulation of other (art) objects that thereby maintain or increase their value. Artists, critics and curators are supposed to play their part. But what

25. See http://www.ipetitions.com/petition/gulflabor/ and the interview with Walid Raad at http://www.art-info.com/news/story/37846/walid-raad-on-why-the-guggenheim-abu-dhabi-must-be-built-on-a-foundation-of-workers-rights/.

if these labourers, these sub-subjects, were placed on the agenda as stubborn and opaque persons, rather than as purely abstract labour power? This political protest created a different kind of visibility by complicating the official image (of, in this case, the Guggenheim). Though this protest was not a work of art per se, in this sense it was most certainly a form of aesthetic praxis.

Who's Building the Guggenheim Abu Dhabi?

HOME PETITION PRESS TIMELINE OF EVENTS POUR PUBLICATION IMMÉDIATE PÉTITION

June 2, 2011: UPDATE on Guggenheim Boycott

GET INVOLVED

We are a coalition of international artists working to ensure that migrant worker rights are protected during the construction and maintenance of the Guggenheim's new branch museum on Saadiyat Island in Abu Dhabi, UAE.

Artists should not be asked to exhibit their work in buildings built on the backs of exploited workers. Those working with bricks and mortar deserve the same kind of respect as those working with cameras and brushes.

Help safeguard migrant workers' rights.

Sign the petition
Email friends

gulflabor [at] gmail [dot] com

BLOGROLL

BREAKING NEW YORK TIMES ARTICLE: Abu Dhabi Guggenheim Faces Protest

Migrant Worker Bus

JUNE 2, 2011: UPDATE ON GUGGENHEIM BOYCOTT

UPDATE 2 June 2011 In May 2011, The Gulflabor coalition submitted to the Guggenheim Foundation and Museum and Tourism Development & Investment Company (TDIC) of Abu Dhabi the following specific recommendations about the selection of an independent monitor: a) No monitor should be selected who has, is, or will be providing services to any contractor ... *Read more*

Filed under *SIGN THE PETITION FOR MIGRANT WORKER RIGHTS*

On Saadiyat Island

GET INVOLVED

Sign the petition
Email friends

gulflabor [at] gmail [dot] com

On Site

```
k     a     t     t     o           m
1     1     1     1     1           1
5     5     7     1     2     5     3
d     r     u     z     i     n     a
h  a  r  r  y  m  o  n  k  e  y
c     o     n     n     o     r     9     8
c     h     i     c     k     e     n
1           9           1     8           9
g           e     h     e     i           m
d           a           n           t           m
z     a     g     r     t     e     b
7     3     4     7     9     8
h           e           s           s
s  i  e  g  h  e  i  l
t     h     o     r     8     8
s  l  o  v  e  n  i  j  a
p  u  e  r  t  o  r  i  c  o
j  o  h  n     1     1     1
```

baldbassist
Zorn39.
Matko
davidoof
madness
andy1488
Reichgeist
ultrassW.P.
Kaman
Dante
plavadivizija
[SEIRYU]
rudolf
skinhead-86
colonelslanders
jegrmajstr88
johnnyozboy
john

```
s l a y e r         8 8
a b c d e f g h i
f u c k y o u       u
c h e l s e a       1
9 3 2 8 1 1         7
b   e   n     o     2
s   h   a m     6   9
6 6 6 8 8 6 6   6
m i k e     8       3
w h i t e p o w e r
1   2   3   4   5   6
k o s a r k a       6
d o m i n i k 8     2
k l e o p a t r a
l a n d s e r       8 8
1 1 0 4   8 7
a   n   d r e   d
c o o l c a t
```

K   a   l   l   e
8 8 \ A r y a n / 1 4
M e l i s s a C A
l e e 1 6 9 0
g o i n g r o t a r y
b   e   n   o
b   r   a   n   d   y
H a b o r y m
H o l y W a r 8 3
d   o   l   f   k   e
R   4   v   3   e   n
b o m b e r 8 8
R   e   i   k
a   d   l   e   r
O d i n   8   8
j e r r e _ 2 8
i n k e d 8 8
b u r n t h e b o o k s

Heath Bunting

Piercing The Veils of Identity Classes

(From hand-eye co-ordination to corporate wealth)

Heath Bunting explores the porosity of borders.
Often performing as an interventionist or
prankster and finding form within everyday
acts of resistance, Bunting's work reaches
its public through systems of documentation
and distribution including photography,
print publishing and the web. Dismantling the
divisions separating art and everyday life,
Bunting prioritizes information and action. His
work is based on creating open and democratic
systems by modifying communication technologies
and social systems.   (Annet Dekker)

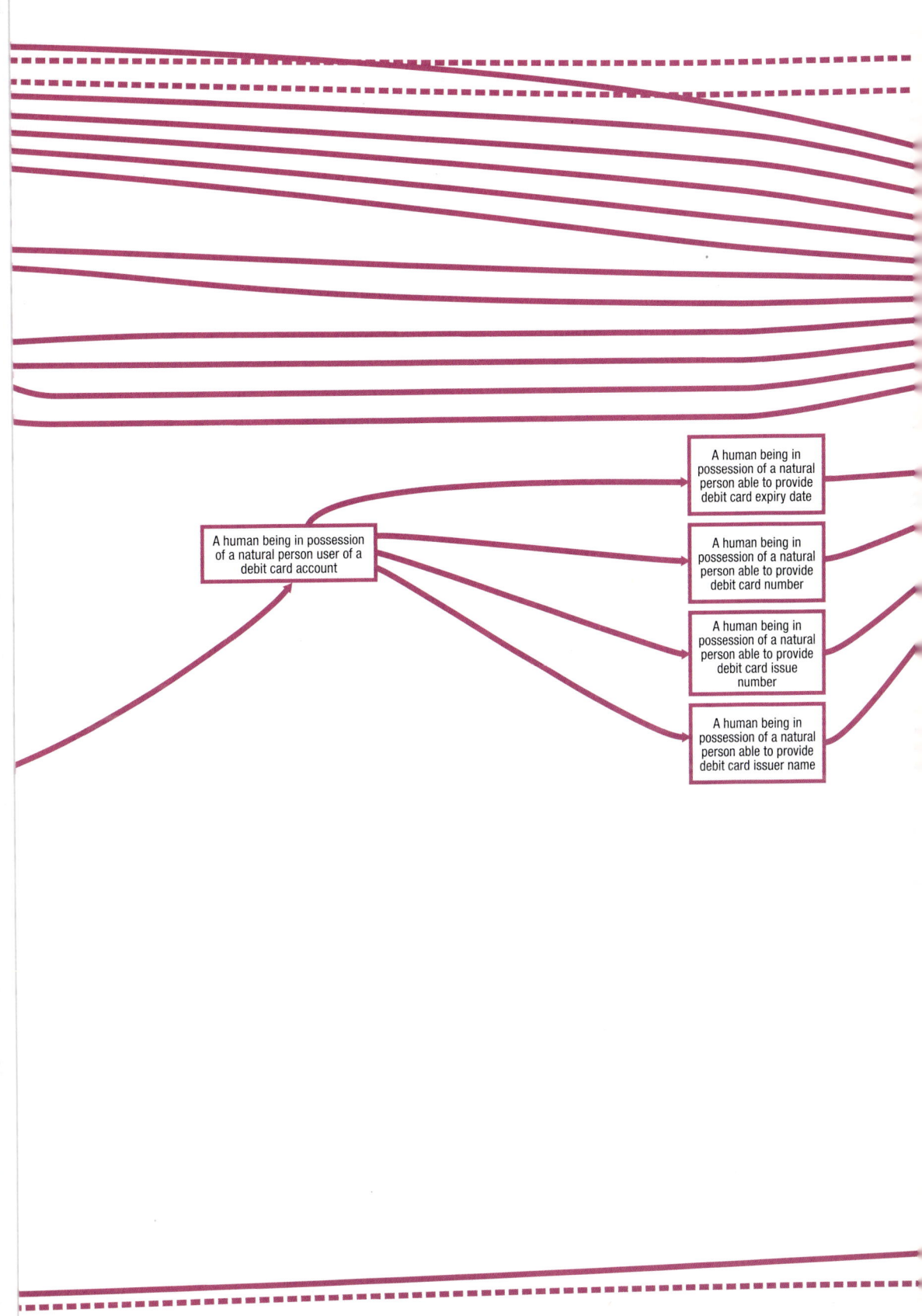

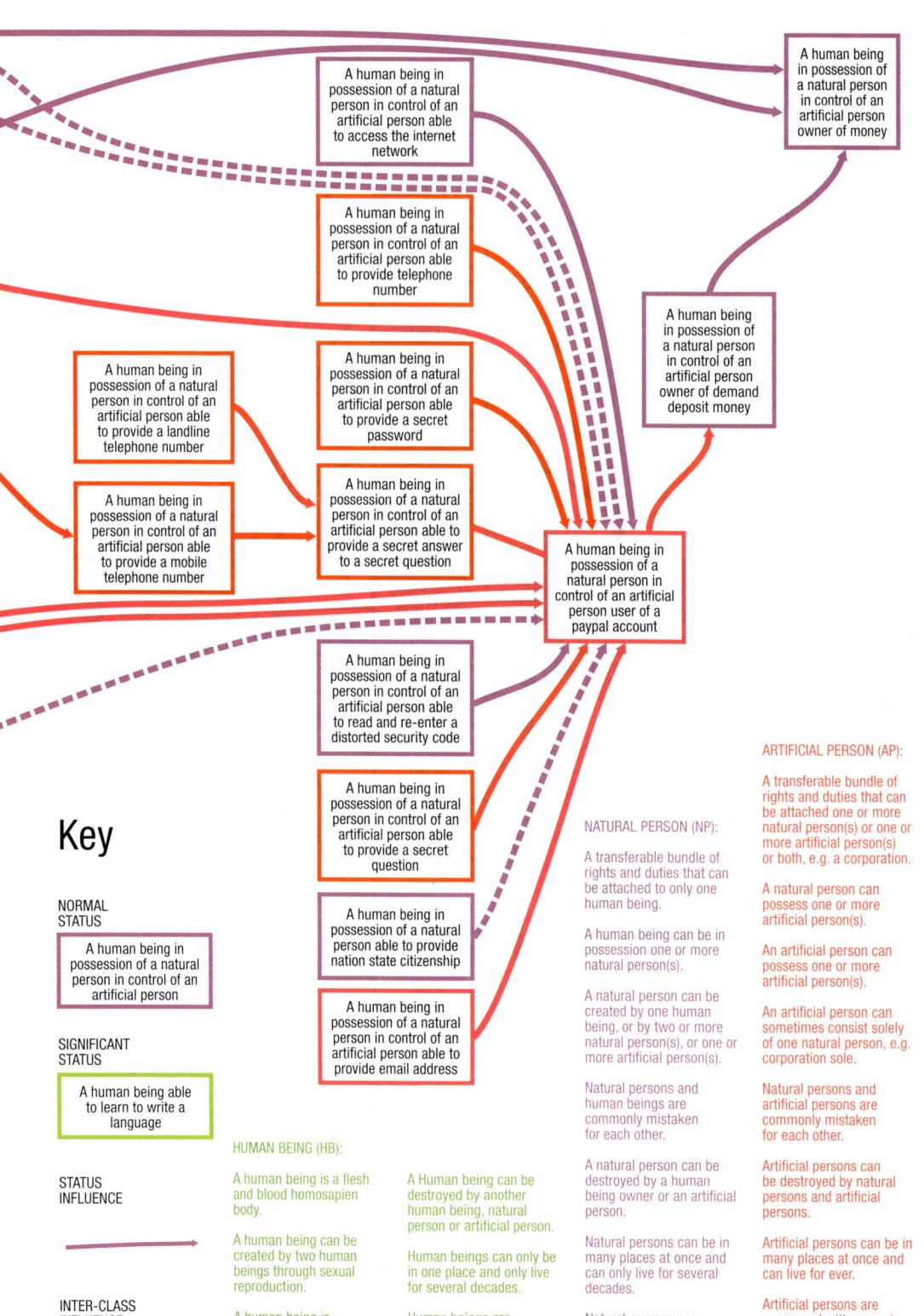

A human being in possession of a natural person in control of an artificial person able to access the internet network

A human being in possession of a natural person in control of an artificial person owner of money

A human being in possession of a natural person in control of an artificial person able to provide telephone number

A human being in possession of a natural person in control of an artificial person owner of demand deposit money

A human being in possession of a natural person in control of an artificial person able to provide a landline telephone number

A human being in possession of a natural person in control of an artificial person able to provide a secret password

A human being in possession of a natural person in control of an artificial person able to provide a mobile telephone number

A human being in possession of a natural person in control of an artificial person able to provide a secret answer to a secret question

A human being in possession of a natural person in control of an artificial person user of a paypal account

A human being in possession of a natural person in control of an artificial person able to read and re-enter a distorted security code

A human being in possession of a natural person in control of an artificial person able to provide a secret question

A human being in possession of a natural person able to provide nation state citizenship

A human being in possession of a natural person in control of an artificial person able to provide email address

Key

NORMAL STATUS

A human being in possession of a natural person in control of an artificial person

SIGNIFICANT STATUS

A human being able to learn to write a language

STATUS INFLUENCE

INTER-CLASS INFLUENCE

HUMAN BEING (HB):

A human being is a flesh and blood homosapien body.

A human being can be created by two human beings through sexual reproduction.

A human being is sometimes created by two human beings with the aid of one or more natural or artificial person(s).

A Human being can be destroyed by another human being, natural person or artificial person.

Human beings can only be in one place and only live for several decades.

Human beings are concerned with survival.

Human beings can possess.

NATURAL PERSON (NP):

A transferable bundle of rights and duties that can be attached to only one human being.

A human being can be in possession one or more natural person(s).

A natural person can be created by one human being, or by two or more natural person(s), or one or more artificial person(s).

Natural persons and human beings are commonly mistaken for each other.

A natural person can be destroyed by a human being owner or an artificial person.

Natural persons can be in many places at once and can only live for several decades.

Natural persons are concerned with property.

Natural persons can own, use and control..

ARTIFICIAL PERSON (AP):

A transferable bundle of rights and duties that can be attached one or more natural person(s) or one or more artificial person(s) or both, e.g. a corporation.

A natural person can possess one or more artificial person(s).

An artificial person can possess one or more artificial person(s).

An artificial person can sometimes consist solely of one natural person, e.g. corporation sole.

Natural persons and artificial persons are commonly mistaken for each other.

Artificial persons can be destroyed by natural persons and artificial persons.

Artificial persons can be in many places at once and can live for ever.

Artificial persons are concerned with property and power.

Artificial persons can own, use and control.

Roel Griffioen

From Glass to One-Way Glass

Shifting Meanings of Transparency, Openness and Privacy in Architecture

Whereas in the 1950s transparency in architecture was considered an unambiguous and politicized ideal, since the advent of the television programme *Big Brother* it has become a paradoxical concept. 'What is transparent for the camera is opaque for the resident,' writes architecture historian Roel Griffioen. Openness and privacy, transparency and opaqueness are intertwined with one another more than ever.

I would say that Bentham was the complement to Rousseau. What in fact was the Rousseauist dream that motivated many of the revolutionaries? It was the dream of a transparent society, visible and legible in each of its parts, the dream of there no longer existing any zones of darkness.
Michel Foucault

Never to my knowledge has the ideal of transparency in architecture been more clearly represented than by the photographer Jan Versnel. The photographs of residential interiors that he made in the 1950s for the Dutch magazine *Goed Wonen* (Good Living) are symbols of modern life in an open, lucid home environment. In these interiors there are hardly any strict divisions; rooms are coupled with one another and solid walls replaced as much as possible by glass walls and doors, giving the impression that the space seems to flow from room to room. Light, modern pieces of furniture figure as the visual components of apt compositions evoking pre-war avant-garde painting and photography. Just as there are no thresholds separating the rooms, the private lives of the various members of the household also commingle. In one photograph, the father of the house is doing his paperwork at the dining room table in total concentration while in the same room his daughter attentively watches a repairman fix the radio. On the balcony, her mother chats with a friend.

Jan Versnel's photographs are not simply photographs; they must be understood as depictions of an educational agenda. The interiors are located in model homes decorated by the Stichting Goed Wonen (Good Living Foundation), an organization set up after the war in the Netherlands by progressive architects, designers, furniture manufacturers and other social reformers who – in their own words – were fighting against 'tastelessness' and whose goal was to promote 'good living for a broadest possible sector of the population'. In a carefully composed *mise en scène*, replete with props and actors, Versnel depicts what this 'good living' entails: living transparently in a transparent house. Family life takes place in the open. The personal worries and cares of individual family members / actors ebb away in the group. All hail to living one's life in the sight of the Other.

This is what I – in concurrence with the utterances of several post-war reconstruction architects and public housing authorities – would like to call the ideal of the glass house. The glass house in itself was not a concrete building assignment, but as an idealized image of a condition of total openness and total transparency, it is implied in much of the architecture and thinking of the 1950s. Nowadays, this ideal, with its patronizing moral and social connotations, seems utopian and hopelessly naive. The glass house has made way for the much more enigmatic image of the 'one-way glass' house, in which concealing has become as important as revealing. On the basis of these two images, I would like to show how concepts such as transparency, openness and privacy have gone adrift over the last half-century.

Transparency as Ideal

The glass house was a bare and empty house, certainly in the eyes of the Dutch in the year 1955. The ideal interiors shown in Versnel's photographs are – to put it disrespectfully – completely purged. The symbols of Dutch middle-class living, such as massive wooden furniture, heavy carpets, crocheted tablecloths and pleated lampshades have been ruthlessly swept from the scene. In the Good Living doctrine, empty houses would lead to clear minds and clean spirits, just as in Thomas More's *Utopia* (1516). In that fictitious realm, there are no 'occasions of corrupting each other, of getting into corners or forming themselves into parties; all men live in full view, so that all are obliged both to perform their ordinary task and to employ themselves well in their spare hours'.[1]

1. Thomas More, *Utopia* (1516, English edition by Cassell & Co, 1901, republished in 2008 by www.forgottenbooks.org), 61-62.

Before the war, Walter Benjamin had already opined that modern architecture's pursuit of light and air would herald the end of the home 'in the old sense of the word', that is to say, the home that put 'security' in the first place. Benjamin praised the modernist ideal of living in a house of glass as a means of moral self-discipline: 'To live in a glass house is a revolutionary virtue par excellence. It is also an intoxication, a moral exhibitionism, that we badly need. Discretion concerning one's own existence, once an aristocratic virtue, has become more and more an affair of petty-bourgeois parvenus.'[2] For Benjamin, the 'old way of living' was equal to a middle-class mentality and class consciousness. Shelter and protection is desired by people who have a fear of society. In an analogous manner, the constructivist El Lissitzky compared steel to the will of the proletariat and glass to its conscience.

2. Walter Benjamin, 'Surrealism: The Last Snapshot of the European Intelligentsia', in Michael William Jennings, Howard Eiland and Gary Smith (eds.), *Walter Benjamin: Selected Writings 1927-1930* (Cambridge, MA: Harvard University Press, 2003), 209.

After the war, the supposed social power of architectural trans-

C. de Vries (interior architect), model home in Slotermeer,
Amsterdam. Published in *Goed Wonen*, August 1956. Photo: Jan
Versnel

The rooms in the model home flow into one another without thresholds between them. When doors are necessary, they are designed to be as transparent as possible. Published in *Goed Wonen*, February 1956. Photo: Jan Versnel

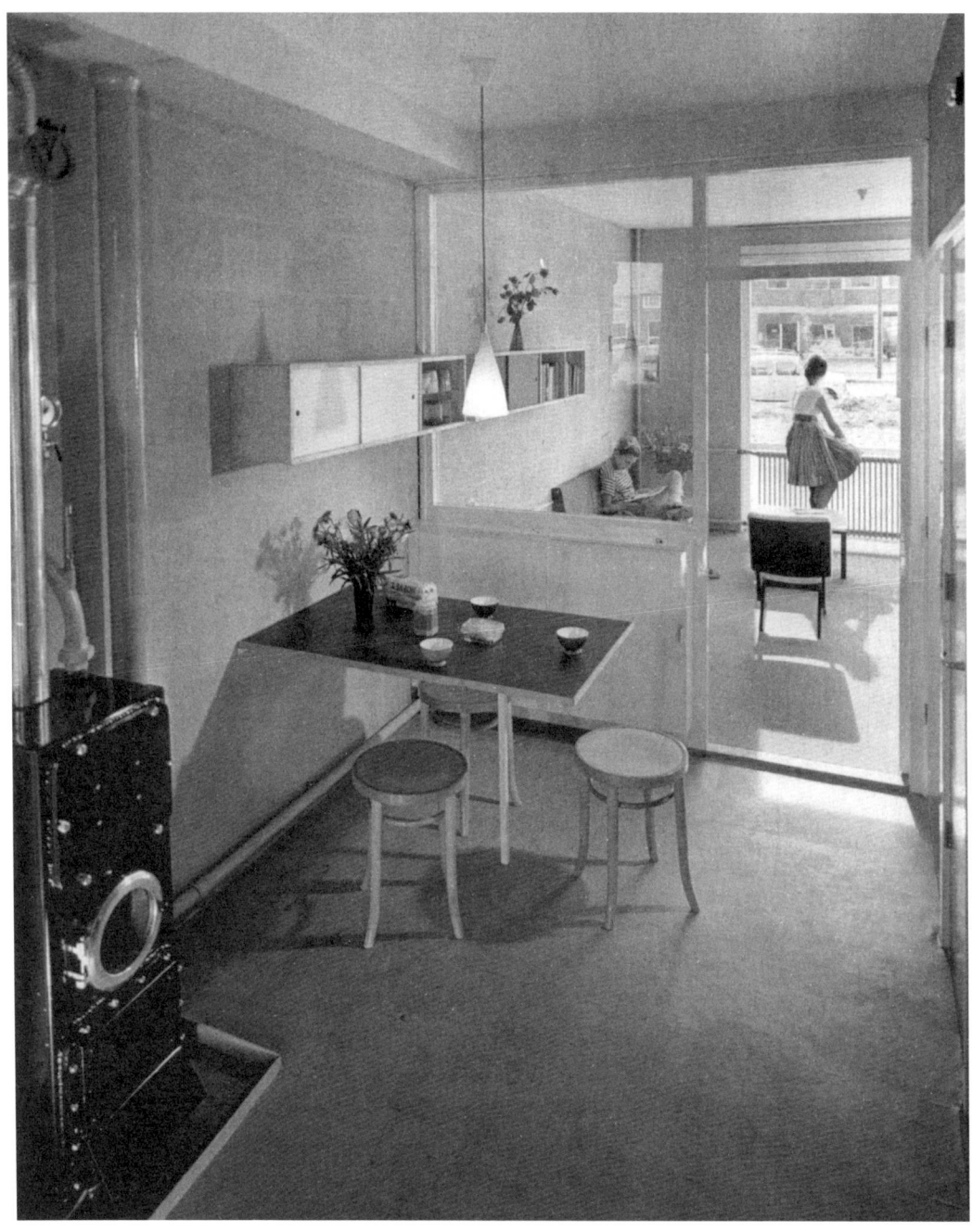

The outside world is part of the interior. Model home in Slotervaart, designed by Kho Liang Ie. Published in *Goed Wonen*, 1960. Photo: Jan Versnel

parency acquired an extra pregnant charge. Transparent space acquired the name of being 'innocent' space, free of pitfalls and secret places; as such, the bare, spacious floor plans in the 1950s were emblematic for a 'new beginning' – in the personal and social sense.[3] Several psychologists proposed in the magazine *Goed Wonen* that a proper residential environment could help people come to terms with the trauma of war. With the spiritual twilight and clandestine nature of the war years still fresh in people's minds, the new architecture moreover radiated the desire for a clearly designed society and a transparent political order. As architect Jaap Bakema wrote in 1947 – in defence of modern residential architecture, nota bene: 'Openness is the condition for democracy.'

3. Henri Lefebvre writes: 'The illusion of transparency goes hand in hand with a view of space as innocent, as free of traps or secret places. Anything hidden or dissimulated – and hence dangerous – is antagonistic to transparency, under whose reign everything can be taken in by a single glance from that mental eye which illuminates whatever it contemplates.' Henri Lefebvre, *The Production of Space* (Malden, USA/Oxford, UK: Wiley-Blackwell, 1991), 28.

Post-war reconstruction architects saw windows as – to paraphrase a statement by Marx – the 'senses' of the home, instruments that brought the marked out domain of family life in contact with the outside world. For example, Bakema proposed that by letting the indoor and outdoor space penetrate one another, life in the home could be part of 'the Big Event': society, the world and even the cosmos.

This aspiration – the abolishment of the boundary line between family and society – can also be seen in Versnel's photographs. The windows at front have no curtains and occupy the entire façade. Family life, formerly often imagined as the bastion of intimacy, is totally exposed to society. The outside world is included in the composition, shown as part of the inside world. The buildings on the other side of the street are visible, framed by the window. Lines of perspective that start in the interior of the dwelling continue through the cityscape without juddering to a halt. 'The home no longer ends at the front door, there to encounter a hostile world,' wrote architect Willem van Tijen. In its austerity and openness, this modern residential architecture referred to a classless society in which it was unnecessary for individuals to seek seclusion, seeing as in society they would encounter the same warmth and safety that was formerly reserved for the home. The model society itself was thus imagined as a society without walls – a glass house.

Already in the 1950s, however, criticism was mounting against the ideal of the glass house. Urban sociologists complained that such houses offered too little sense of security. These critics sooner associated openness with social control, surveillance and government interference than with autonomy and democracy. Not transparency but its opposite, privacy, was what they associated with freedom – more specifically, 'the freedom to determine one's own life'. They felt that the lack of lockable rooms in the house and all that glass would act as a check on the inhabitants' right to self development. In the critics' experience, the glass house was in reality a see-through straitjacket.

Nowadays, anyone who walks through an arbitrary redevelopment district in the Netherlands will get the impression that the bankruptcy of the glass-house ideal is definitive. Under the banner of urban renewal, entire neighbourhoods have been torn down and replaced by introverted types of dwellings, housing blocks closed to the outside world and enclave-like 'residential domains', islands in the urban fabric. Open housing as an emblem of social transparency has been defeated by the 'my home is my castle' ideal, in which the home is the antithesis of society. Privacy is deemed more important than openness. Those who can afford it move into an enclave, shut themselves off from a world that is identified with danger, animosity and inconvenience.

Shifting Meanings

The metaphor of total transparency has always been Janus-faced, with on the one side the promise of freedom, equality and democracy, and on the other the nightmare of totalitarian surveillance and loss of individuality. In the classic dystopias in literature, the 'public' aspect imposed by the system is the most important instrument of coercion and disciplining. In the 'One State' in Yevgeny Zamyatin's novel *We*, the 'crystallization of life' has been made the highest objective.[4] For the citizens of this dictatorship, who truly live in glass houses, the hour for sex is the only time that the shades can be drawn. In Ayn Rand's *Anthem* as well, 'none among men may be alone, ever and at any time, for this is the great transgression and the root of all evil'.[5] So you can roughly say that what symbolizes a kind of paradisiacal condition for the community-minded represents a hell for liberals, who see the citizen as an autonomous subject whose principal right is that of self development.

4. Yevgeny Zamyatin, *We* (New York: Harper Collins, 1972), 24.

5. Ayn Rand, *Anthem* (New York: New American Library, 1976), 12.

Yet this classic dichotomy no longer appears tenable. Openness and privacy, visibility and shelter, transparency and opacity are concepts that have begun to shift. The revival of the 'my home is my castle' ideal, for example, has not been accompanied by a lessening of surveillance. As paradoxical as it may seem, the increase of privacy requires greater transparency. However, the difference with the glass house model is that this transparency only works in one direction. Camera surveillance, gatekeeper policies and videophones are the most visible indicators of this one-way visibility. More subtle forms are the closed or half-closed residential blocks in which the collective can keep an eye on the semi-public space (the courtyard or inner garden). Supervision does not take place from one central panoptical Eye, but from the totality of all the residents, who can watch over the semi-public space with hundreds of pairs of eyes at once without having to leave the comfortable protection of their own homes.

The ideal of the glass house may be dead and buried, but it has reincarnated in a new form. For lack of a better term, I call this the 'one-way glass house'. A one-way glass is a material that expresses the blurring of concepts indicated above: it gives the possibility of seeing without being seen. This complexity can be further enriched with the one-way glass house's prototype, namely the 'house' in which the first *Big Brother* series was filmed in 1999. This is the very picture of openness and transparency, albeit in a totally different way than the modernists had predicted.

It is no exaggeration to state that *Big Brother* signalled the breakthrough of reality TV in the West. This formula conceived by Endemol was first tried out in the Netherlands and then exported to almost 70 countries. The premiering season was broadcast on Veronica from 16 September to 30 December 1999 (a total of 106 days). The formula was simple. Eight candidates were put into a house, with one person being 'voted away' each week, until after about 100 days three participants were left over. From these three, the television audience chose the winner.

More sensational than this game formula was the fact that the participants were continually filmed throughout their stay and that they were completely closed off from the outside world. All of the ethical, psychological and dramatic aspects of this programme have already been extensively discussed in the literature on the subject, so I would like to limit myself to its 'architecture', in other words, the physical setting for the TV formula. The house in which the first season of *Big Brother* was shot was specially built for that purpose, at the edge of Almere, a location that was chosen because the residents would have the feeling of being 'on a drilling rig in the ocean'.[6] The living quarters comprised a house with 145 m² of floor space and a 260 m² garden. This dwelling, a space that was artificially shuttered but visible to the public via the cameras, was the stage on which the participants engaged in 'reality'. The space was physically very enclosed, enclave-like, inward looking, but at the same time completely transparent. With 24 fixed cameras, every nook and cranny of this interior was made visible to the television viewer. The layout, the cameras and the interior design formed a unit that could not be dismantled. The participants were not allowed to move the furniture an inch, on penalty of being thrown out. Even the direction in which the participants slept – from the head to the foot of the bed – was especially geared to the camera positions.

6. Rentsje de Gruyter, 'Op de kaart: Almere', *NRC Handelsblad*, 2 December 1999.

Screened off from the field of vision of the participants and the television viewers was an extensive architectural programme that facilitated the interior's visual transparency. A production unit with 162 m² of floor space – thus larger than the house itself – was built next to the house. A look at the floor plan shows that a secret infrastructure was moulded around the interior revealed by the cameras. Lying in two cross-shaped corridors are rails upon which cameras are ridden past the most important rooms, which are purposely linked to the cross: the living room, the kitchen, a confession room (the diary room) and the two bedrooms. The cameras can look inside through one-way transparent strips – indeed, one-way glass mirrors. What is transparent for the camera is opaque for the residents. The 'architecture' built up out of sound and image is completely transparent, while the physical architecture is stratified and mystifying.

The Stimulation of Behaviour

In the topological sense, the *Big Brother* house is a kind of cuckoo chick in a family in which community spirit is the norm. Of note, for example, is its relation with the communal houses that the Russian constructivists designed during the interwar period, residential complexes in which the possibilities for seclusion were reduced to zero through the architecture. Like the workers in utopian Soviet designs, the residents of *Big Brother* slept with others in the same room, the men and women apart. Personal possessions were limited – Benjamin's statements that transparency is the enemy of secrets and property is as applicable to the *Big Brother* house as it is to the radical residential experiments in Russia. Indeed, the openness was carried even further in the temporary complex in Almere. Even in places where it was possible for the housemates to be alone (in the toilet and shower) the television viewer's technical eye was present.

For the constructivists, this architectural model was a symbol of 'social hygiene', of order and community spirit. For the makers of *Big Brother*, it embodied the exact opposite. The openness of the house was supposed to function as a catalyser for Big Feelings. The aim of the architecture was not to make individuals lose themselves in the collective, but to splinter the collective into an assembly of individuals. The idea was that when people are so cooped up in an apparatus of boredom and gossip, they eventually must reveal their true nature. When reasonableness is cast aside, the individual emerges. The competitive element of the programme destroys even the most persistent remnants of unity and solidarity. Contrived with the help of weekly assignments prescribed by *Big Brother* – read: the director's unit next door – the weekly round of elimination and the televised confession in the diary room was a quick washing machine cycle for hyper-individuality. For this reason, the producers chose a special palette of candidates for the first season in Germany, including 'a lesbian, a boy with earrings and tattoos, and a girl who works in the telephone sex industry'. The goal, according to the producers: 'More fights in the house.'[7]

7. Jochen van Barschot, 'Du bist nicht allein. Meer ruzie en meer seks in Duitse versie Big Brother', *NRC Handelsblad*, 25 February 2000.

As is known, *Big Brother* is named after the tyrannizing System in George Orwell's *1984* – another dystopia in which openness and transparency are described as methods of suppression. Orwell's Big Brother uses surveillance as a means of colonizing the individual's private space and enforcing disciplined behaviour. By contrast, what is stimulated by means of surveillance in the *Big Brother* programme is abnormal behaviour. The presence of cameras – and thus viewers – titillates the participants' egos. In the vacuumed interior of the house, their prickled egos run into one another every other minute, resulting in explosions of Big Feelings (love, hate). Their exhibitionism is fed by our voyeurism. Why do we want to peek through the one-way mirror?

Big Brother house, from the *Big Brother* series produced by
Endemol, broadcast on Veronica from 16 September to 30 December
1999.

Entrance

View of interior through two-way mirror

Kippenhok

Garden

Terrace

Koelkast

Kitchen

Living Room

Camera
Space

Eettafel

Open
haard

Aquarium

Verwenkast

Diary
Room

Camera
Space

Women's
Bedroom

Men's
Bedroom

Camera
Space

Shower

WC

Camera	
Camera-rail	
Door	
Two-way Mirror	
Window	

Ambiguous

Transparency has lost its clarity as a metaphor. Social theorization can no longer be captured in a crystal-clear architectural image like the glass house. Whereas for political decision-making, WikiLeaks or the financial system, total transparency can still function as an ideal – even though this is increasingly becoming problematical – the storage of telecom information, preventive frisking, camera surveillance and so forth have a decidedly dystopian component. Concepts like openness and privacy – at one time antipodal – have become interchangeable. The houses that we are designing and building today are as far removed as possible from the glass house ideal of the 1950s. We move into an apartment in a brand-new housing block whose façade refers to the crisis architecture of the 1930s, or a monumental building in the classic style of 'our' Golden Age, or even better, a closed domain whose inhospitality is emphasized by mettlesome corner turrets with battlements and a veritable moat. In this fort of intimacy, we find diversion by watching people on TV who have voluntarily locked themselves up in public view. Through the television programme *Big Brother*, we are offered up for consumption a kind of pasteurized version of precisely what we with great difficulty have tried to ban from our own social environment: insecurity, uncertainty, the unknown.[8]

8. Slavoj Žižek brings up interesting and more existential reasons for our penchant for reality TV. He speaks of a tragicomic reversal of the panopticum model, whereby the 'observed always' is turned into a positive, perhaps even intoxicating aspect of life. *Big Brother* and its countless spin-offs and successors are symptoms of this reversal. Žižek even suggests that we meanwhile have all become actors in a reality soap opera, because we live in the awareness of the possibility of a panoptic Eye that follows all of our actions. 'What if Big Brother was already here, as the (imagined) Gaze for whom I was doing things, whom I tried to impress, to seduce, even when I was alone?' Slavoj Žižek, 'Big Brother, or, the Triumph of the Gaze over the Eye', in: Thomas Levin (ed.), *CTRL [SPACE]: Rhetorics of Surveillance from Bentham to Big Brother* (Karlsruhe: ZKM, 2002), 224-227.

Lieven De Cauter, Ru
Roo and Karel Vanhae
(eds.), *Art and Activis*
Age of Globalization

Merijn Oudenampsen

In evolutionary biolog
cial place is reserved f
island dweller. Becaus
relative isolation of isl
evolution of the speci
on them took a remar
turn. Safe from the th
the mainland, from th
tential struggle with tl
living there, island dw
developed the most p
characteristics and sp
lar superfluities. They
extremely focused spe
and often also noncor
eccentrics. Languid, r
giants and jaunty bird
to fly survived for mil
thanks to their isolatio
the inevitable momen
the invasion came fro
mainland, and the spe
and eccentrics proved
less to defend themse
 The contemporary
an island dweller. But
long was a world unto itself
can no longer be just that. The
arts are under fire. Dramatic
cutbacks in culture are in the
works. The art world's attempt
to defend itself comes across as
shaky and ill at ease; its argu-
ments hardly find a response
beyond its own circles. The ap-
peal to civilization, the shared
message of the art protests thus
far, only confirms the cliché.

*Community Art. The Politics of
Trespassing* (Valiz Publishers);
the first volume in NAi
Publishers' Reflect series,
Nieuw Engagement; and the
recent tract on cultural activism by BAVO, *Too Active to Act*
(Valiz) and it would appear
there is a good basis for carrying out the discussion on
an engaged art practice to full
satisfaction. The disputed char-

their performative undermining of the visual idiom of the
war on terror, about the way in
which Christoph Schlingensief
used his body to analyse the
social condition, about the
Parisian flash-mob campaigns
to re-conquer public space
from the advertising pillars,
about artistic inquiry into colo-
nial historiography in Belgium.
We read about uncompromis-

ing American underground cinema, about a director who is principally objected to a breakthrough, about Renzo Marten's *Enjoy Poverty*, that most painful of attacks on the political economy of development aid, about theatre makers who are supporting the *sans papiers* in a difficult process of self-questioning instead of affirmation, about Mexican-American gay performers who attempt to penetrate the armoured identities and intensified border controls of the USA after 9/11.

You might expect that such an impressive series of projects would be accompanied by an impassioned introduction, a call to take up artistic arms. And apparently that was the editors' original intention: a guidebook for new generations on the necessity of subversion, how to turn the complex and problematic tension between activism and art into something productive. Something strange must have happened. In*stead*, the volume exudes a feeling of nostalgia and depression. Lieven De Cauter's introduction can best be read as a funeral speech for artistic protest and aesthetic subversion. After this interment, De Cauter calls for defensive and affirmative action – that is to say, defence of what we still have left: human rights, the welfare state, the environment. In Karel Vanhaesebrouck's essay we read that art's role

in portraying a different society no longer matters, now that change is no longer a real possibility. From now on, we should focus on the most prosaic: human survival. We find the same depressing approach taken by Rosi Braidotti, whose article seems to have provided the inspiration for the strange jump from subversion to affirmation that De Cauter makes in the introduction. Mass political activism, according to Braidotti, has nowadays been replaced by 'processes of public and collective mourning'. Not so strange, then, that her article reads like a therapeutic session to reconcile participants in aesthetic resistance with their losses, only to subsequently refer them to the affirmation of their 'non-unitary subject'. And then there's Ruben de Roo, who in a peculiar manner manages to read *The Author as Producer*, Walter Benjamin's key text on artistic engagement, as a call for individualistic art, as much as possible devoid of any ideological inclination. It is difficult to misread Benjamin as badly as that.

The strange thing about the editors' 'affirmative' approach is first of all that the power of modern art lies precisely in its tension with the existing order of things, in the depiction of possible worlds. We don't need art for propagating the here and now, we can

simply open the newspaper for that. Secondly, their approach seems to be in open contradiction with the majority of the art projects discussed in the book: aesthetic subversion is not dead – it is simply buried alive in De Cauter's introduction. Subversion and imagination are also abundant in the other theoretical contributions in *Art & Activism*. Brian Holmes provides a subversive cross between the philosophy of Deleuze and Guattari and cybernetics. Rudi Laermans argues for commonalism, a new politics of the common, and John Jordan talks about his laboratory of the insurrectionary imagination. Gie Goris and Christophe van Eecke conclude with a ruggedly inflammatory tone. Those who want to change something, we read, must take risks: *Change something. Make a difference. Go screw some government tonight.*

As such, the book somewhat manically totters between desperate depression and cheerful agitation, between introverted mourning and high-spirited determination. Perhaps this contradiction is precisely what makes the book more than a good collection of prominent political art projects and penetrating theoretical essays. It makes this volume a faithful reflection of the contemporary state of mind.

Paul De Bruyne and Pascal Gielen (eds.), *Community Art: The Politics of Trespassing*

Amsterdam, Valiz, 2011, ISBN 978-90-78088-50-9, 374 p., € 19.90

Ilse van Rijn

Community Art: The Politics of Trespassing is a collection of essays, interviews and reports compiled by Pascal Gielen and Paul De Bruyne within the framework of the Arts *in* Society chair at the Fontys School of Fine and Performing Arts, Tilburg. The chair's research group investigates the relations between societal changes and artistic creation. Gielen and De Bruyne are respectively lecturer and co-lecturer of the chair. As part of their ongoing research, they previously published *Being an Artist in Post-Fordist Times* (2009). In the introduction to their present book, the editors explain that *Community Art* is a response to hypothetical questions from the public on the launching of *Being an Artist*. At that time, they suggested that an acceptance of the results of the present 'post-Fordist' era could be seen within community art in particular. On the one hand this was evidenced by the revival of community art and, on the other, by the forms and functions these art practices assume. As such, artists involved in community art projects appear to be cursed with an extremely 'flexible' and opportunistic attitude.

The complexity of every community art project, Gielen and De Bruyne subsequently propose, is determined by the oscillation between 'the com-mon' and the 'individual'. The first concept was theoretically strongly developed in the 1980s, among others by Paolo Virno, Michael Hardt and Antonio Negri. The individual is embraced both by the art practices occurring since the late nineteenth century and by the market thinking that has arisen during the same time. The editors attempt to clarify the complicated, even para-doxical, position of community art between these two poles by including a multitude of subjective positions and inter-pretations in addition to more theoretical contributions that expound upon or question the conceptual grounds of com-munity art.

The book comprises four sections and an epilogue. 'Definitions', with which the book begins, opens with two essays by Gielen and De Bruyne themselves, in which the insights acquired in *Being an Artist* are further worked out and translated into models for measuring the social or ar-tistic 'success' of a community art project. De Bruyne devel-oped the 'Brown Scale', with which the level of virtuosity, autonomy or collective nature of a work of art's produc-tion can be charted, among other things. The works of the Brussels music collective MET-X, which according to De Bruyne is one of the forerun-ners of community art, are used to test the model.

In 'Mapping Community Art', Gielen starts from the idea that all art is relational. Furthermore, he proposes that aesthetics and ethics are antip-odal. Although most projects are somewhere between these two poles, art works can be categorized as 'auto-relational' (aimed at themselves) or 'allo-relational' (aimed at the other). Both extremes include 'subver-sive' and 'digestive' projects. In practice, however, the distinc-tion is not always so clear, as can be seen by Gielen's exam-ples and by the essays in the anthology. In theory, the au-thor gives the term 'digestive' to art projects that confirm the dominant prevailing norms, values and customs, and that promote social integration. By way of illustration, he exam-ines Rémy Zaugg's *Le lavoir de Blessey* (2007) as a case of 'digestive auto-relational art'. Zaugg's work in the hamlet of Blessey in France's Bourgogne was realized on commission from the mediating agency Les Nouveaux Commanditaires. It came about after a long process of negotiation and compromise. Remarkably, the author subsequently typifies the work as a 'real Zaugg', without describing it in artistic terms. Setting aside the ques-tion of whether it's even desir-able to measure works of art in statistical terms, or whether Zaugg's work can be labelled 'community art', as Gielen himself endorses, the summary explanation in the artistic sense above all expresses the author's position: community art must be understood in a social context. And: social relevance and artistic urgency rule one another out.

The fact that the explanation of what is still always called a 'balancing act between ethics and aesthetics' rests on empirical data, and on previously articulated concepts, becomes clear in the second, third and fourth sections of *Community Art*. Theatre maker Bart Van Nuffelen, for example, discusses his play *De vernissage* by the Flemish MartHa!tentatief, based on experiences with drug-using habitués of the Coninckplein in Antwerp. The artistic qualities of *De vernissage* were no less than the social emancipatory success of the work. In many community art projects, however, this balance is lacking, according to Van Nuffelen. Particularly the considerable subsidies that have been granted to 'social artistic projects' in Belgium since the 1990s do harm to artistic quality. Art is all too often instrumentalized, and its critical potential neutralized, by allocating it a place. Prior to this, Gielen and De Bruyne rightly warned against this strategy, which Herbert Marcuse described as 'repressive tolerance'.

During his visit to Alert Bay, a little town lying off the northwest coast of North America, composer and researcher Hein Schoer concludes that it is not always possible to see artistic projects and artistic enterprises separately from a specific culture and its preservation. Half of the 550 residents of Alert Bay are of Caucasian descent, the other half belong to the Namgis tribe. Woodcutting determines the identity of the community and gives it expression. And in a potlatch ceremony, social positions are transferred and claimed through the trade and distribution of handmade goods.

Alida Neslo, director of DasArts, experienced that, thanks to the concept of *alakondre*, a bridge can be built between different peoples and mentalities. The word, originating from the Surinamese language of Sranan, means something like 'the search for the other, for whatever differs from your own beliefs, your own appearance, your own view of reality'.

Her observations are surprisingly similar to those of Antonio Negri in his perspective on 'the common'. Contranatural love and solidarity fulfil an important role in this, explains Negri in an interview with Gielen and Sonja Lavaert. Community spirit arises through an encounter between contrary passions and conflict.

In the various essays, interviews and reports in *Community Art*, the art projects bearing that name are particularly understood from the point of view of their social relevance. The book above all makes a contribution to reflection on the communal from an ethical perspective. Although the existence of an aesthetic component in community art projects is recognized, a needed discussion about a possible interpretation of this is almost painstakingly avoided. The only author who defends the aesthetic aspect does so without substantive argument. That is a pity, especially because the projects discussed are nevertheless presented as art. What's more, the multiplicity and variety of disciplines presented in this compilation prevent the reader from in any way understanding a community art project in its artistic form. The geopolitical dispersion of the projects contributes to this: dance from the USA (Lionel Popkin) and China (Zhang Changcheng), circus from Sweden (Tilde Björfors), video art from Indonesia (Miguel Escobar Varela), to name but a few examples. The question then arises: What is the motivation behind these choices? The compilers of *Community Art* seem to be saying that in community art projects in particular it is impossible to create a new kind of social involvement by means of aesthetics. Virno's notion of 'Dismeasure', for example, examined in *Being an Artist* as theoretical support of that possibility, is no longer discussed in this book. This above all makes *Community Art. The Politics of Trespassing* an endorsement of the statement that Gielen formulated in his own essay: social relevance and artistic urgency rule one another out.

Paul O'Neill and Claire
Doherty (eds.), *Locating
the Producers: Durational
Approaches to Public Art*

Jeroen Boomgaard

Amsterdam, Valiz,
ISBN 978-90-78088-51-6,
288 p., €19.90

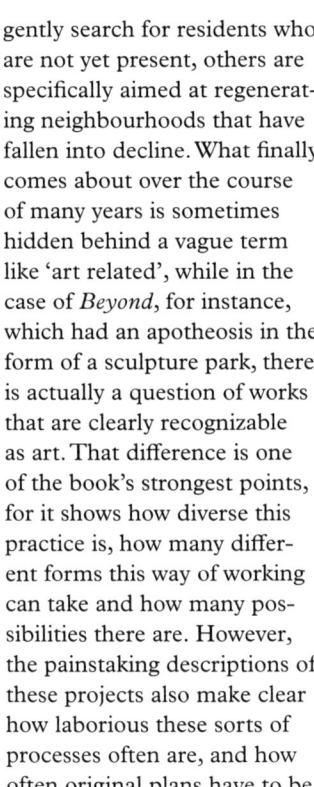

Temporariness is one of the most successful notions of the past decades. The temporary presence of art, in contrast to its isolated confinement in museum collections or its permanent occupation of public space in stone or bronze, appears to have more of a chance of becoming part of our daily lives. At first, this temporary presence focused on unusual spots outside the art circuit. Armed with maps and descriptions, large groups of art lovers visited districts and buildings in which art had never before been shown. But this form of temporariness, already suspect because of its affinity with spectacle, definitively lost the greatest part of its attractiveness when it was realized that most of the interventions not only took little interest in the grudging decor of the local population, but that the artists hastily flown in and out were also not much more than workers available at the command of the big neoliberal boss.

Since then, the notion of temporariness has been stretched. A model that seems to overcome the objections, certainly when giving art a place in a community as a part of social processes is involved, is a combination of short-term projects within a longer time framework. This fits in with the realization that, while routines and traditions do exist, life does not stand still. Although

daily life for most of us takes place according to fixed patterns, it is filled with chance occurrences, disruptions and changes that simply go with living in a community. At the same time, however, sweeping change is a lengthy process, and a short term project, no matter how participatory, often is no more than a fleeting diversion from daily worries.

Locating the Producers revolves around five projects that take this model as their point of departure: *The Blue House* by Jeanne van Heeswijk in Amsterdam's IJburg district, *Creative Egremont* by the Grizedale Arts organization in Cumbria, England, *Trekroner Art Plan* in Roskilde, Denmark, the *Edgware Road Project* in London and *Beyond* in Leidsche Rijn near Utrecht in the Netherlands. All of these projects are of long duration and characterized by a great involvement with the area in which they occur. Moreover, they strive to collaborate with the residents/users. And all of the selected projects are supported by an artist/organizer/curator who guarantees their long duration and forms the permanent factor underlying the changing and shifting layer of temporary works, processes and projects. But there the similarity ends. For while some of these ventures take place in newly developed areas where the organization has to dili-

gently search for residents who are not yet present, others are specifically aimed at regenerating neighbourhoods that have fallen into decline. What finally comes about over the course of many years is sometimes hidden behind a vague term like 'art related', while in the case of *Beyond*, for instance, which had an apotheosis in the form of a sculpture park, there is actually a question of works that are clearly recognizable as art. That difference is one of the book's strongest points, for it shows how diverse this practice is, how many different forms this way of working can take and how many possibilities there are. However, the painstaking descriptions of these projects also make clear how laborious these sorts of processes often are, and how often original plans have to be revised.

The book was written from the inside. The team that did the research, headed up by Paul O'Neill, followed the projects very closely, asked difficult questions, and in that way had an influence on how things went. Such an approach is also fitting for this form of art. Work that takes time to develop, in which research and process development play an important role, cannot simply be described or analysed from a distance. In that sense, the book is just as post-critical as the art production it scrutiniz-

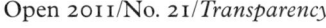

es. The projects want to make a contribution, each in their own manner, to the place they focus upon. In doing so, they maintain a precarious balance between adaptation and agony, but usually there is no question of taking a critical outsider's position. The pursuance of embedding does not permit that. When it does occur, for example with the exhibition 'In Pursuit of Happiness', which is part of *Beyond*, contact with the local population is totally absent.

The book also pays somewhat for that lack of distance. Although a number of short essays by Mick Wilson, Dave Beech and Ned Rossiter comment on some of the central principles of this approach, the book primarily rests on the descriptions of the projects. Owing to O'Neill's understanding and his feeling for nuances and problems, while at the same time attempting to avoid the all-too-cheerful prose with which organizers keep their subsidizers satisfied, the sharpness and pleasure are lacking. The texts read like an exhaustive account of an extremely long party that the reader has nothing to do with. Visually, too, except for a CD-ROM with all of the works

of *Beyond*, the book does not have much to offer. That is a predominant characteristic of this sort of lengthy project, oriented especially towards participation. If you were not there in person, you have to make do with the photographs, and they generally show, as the highpoint, a number of people sitting around a table, deeply concentrated on the question of how to go on from here.

That raises the question of what actually remains of these long-running ventures. What has happened, what has been accomplished, what changes have taken place? The effects, and certainly the affects, are difficult to measure. In his essay, Mick Wilson offers the possibility that this is about 'discursive exhibitions' that do not end with the ending of the project but keep developing over the course of time. That might be so, but I wouldn't know exactly who this 'discursive exhibition' is meant for. While the happenings, events, processions, parades, art manifestations and gatherings do their best to be as accessible and understandable as possible, the considerations and intentions that underlie them are quite impenetrable. Just as with many forms of artistic

research, the increased servitude of the artistic work seems to have to be compensated for by an equally great increase of 'discursive distance'.

The question of what these projects actually produce is not so much aimed at their tangible results in the sense of successful works of art or communities charged with new energy. The criteria for this are still lacking, and perhaps that question is also not the most important. However, it is interesting to know whether the objective that motivates these projects has been realized. For if this is about giving art a different place in the community, letting it play a different role in the daily lives of groups and individuals for whom art usually does not have much to offer, then the result should be a recognition of that new position. If art chooses the ethical principle of wanting to make a contribution to the daily struggle of existence, then you may expect that something like this is also seen as a contribution by society. For the time being, however, in the Netherlands at least, there doesn't seem to be any open, social appreciation for this intensive and lengthy effort on the part of art and artists.

Maria Hlavajova, Simon
Sheikh and Jill Winder (eds.),
*On Horizons: A Critical Reader
in Contemporary Art*

Utrecht/Rotterdam, BAK/
post editions, 2011,
ISBN 978-94-6083-037-2,
242 p., € 24.-

Ilse van Rijn

On Horizons, the fourth critical reader published by Utrecht's centre for contemporary art, BAK, comprises a selection of texts in which an attempt is made to study the present 'Western' condition in art and society on the basis of the concept of 'horizon', according to the editors. This reader is a continuation of the theme presented in the autumn of 2010 at BAK in the group exhibition 'Vectors of the Possible', curated by Simon Sheikh, and at the second Former West Research Congress, 'On Horizons: Art and Political Imagination', which took place in Istanbul and was organized in collaboration with SKOR. The compilers of this volume, Maria Hlavajova, Simon Sheikh and Jill Winder, pose the question: Is the notion of 'horizon', in the philosophical and artistic sense, an instrument that can be used to reformulate the relation between art and politics? Can we create possibilities for artistic practices and political projects by breathing new life into the concept of 'horizon', repositioning it in today's world ruled by neoliberalism?

In this book, artistic and art historical contributions by Sheikh, T.J. Demos, Hito Steyerl, Ultra-red and others are grouped around the philosophical essays of Ernesto Laclau and Peter Osborne. T.J. Demos signals a tendency he calls 'curatorial utopianism'.

A renewed engagement with utopian ideas is discernible in exhibitions, observes Demos. In art institutes, an attempt is being made to escape the grip of the existing context through a willingness to change the economic and political situation. Attractive alternatives for the political status quo are being created. Demos examines how these are being realized on the basis of the nomadic project *Utopia Station* (2003-present), the exhibition 'Forms of Resistance' (2007-2008) in the Van Abbemuseum and the 11th Biennial of Istanbul (2009).

'Forms of Resistance' was primarily a research exhibition, which lacked dynamics and dialogue and was difficult to fathom for non-initiated visitors. In 'Utopia Station', 'utopia' is used as a catalyser so as to study that concept in a non-hierarchical, decentralized manner. Whereas both of these projects tended to degenerate into a non-place for institutional or discursive invisibility, the curators of WDW/What, How and for Whom?, responsible for the 11th Biennial of Istanbul, best understood that risk, according to Demos, and also turned it to their advantage. Polarizing political statements, which cannot be excluded in a 'utopian' exhibition project, frighten away stakeholders in the economic and political sense. WDW utilized a pluralistic agenda, with which

it was able to break into the neoliberal system. The biennial accepted co-financing from the industrial conglomerate Koç Holding, for example, without relinquishing its demand for the possibility of applying a Brechtian aesthetics to contemporary art. The often heard criticism that this approach would undermine the credibility of the biennial with regard to content is too easy, argues Demos. As he prefers to see it, existing systems are 'functionalized' in this manner, so that art can be thought of beyond its form as an overall spectacle or gross entertainment.

In her notes, artist Sharon Hayes analyses what she calls 'arresting images' step-by-step. These are images of, for instance, important protests, physical 'acts of resistance' or acts of violence against the state that attempt to disrupt the prevailing narrative in which 'historical time' is philosophically interpreted as progressive. Hayes cites what have proven to be the visionary statements of Malcolm X uttered before he was murdered in 1965 as an example of arresting images. And she refers to Robert Smithson's 'nonsites', places that in the form of photographs or films are directly connected with a specific time and place, without actually being those places. Yet these non-sites-as-images bind us to themselves, says Hayes.

So, she wonders, might images be able, like Malcolm X's words, to create spatial expectations, to bring about a future experience?

Hayes inverts the conceptual alliance of the two historical categories of 'horizons of expectation' and 'spaces of experience' postulated by Reinhart Koselleck, the German theoretical historian. Koselleck historicized the concept of 'horizon', which already had a longer tradition in philosophy, relates Peter Osborne. 'Horizon' is connected with expectations. At the beginning of the twentieth century, Edmund Husserl redefined Augustine's theological implications of this concept, resulting in a phenomenological description of a 'horizon of expectation'. This is characterized by a 'determinable indeterminateness'; it is veiled in mist and can never be completely determined, but is inevitably there. According to Husserl, explains Osborne, a certain movement is inherent on the horizon. The horizon forms a naive and natural constituting facet of the human position. The horizon precedes reflection and simultaneously defines, in its indeterminateness, human finiteness. Martin Heidegger adopted the possibilities and expectations sketched by Husserl, adding the notion of time as an existential, ontologically fundamental concept. In doing so, he set on edge the definition of what 'possibilities' or 'expectations' are. If you expect something, then you are waiting for the actualization of 'something'. You therefore are ready to have 'it', for after all you are anticipating 'it'. So-called

'possibilities' therefore do not exist. Conversely, Heidegger's concept of 'anticipatoriness' (*Vorlaufigkeit*), includes human existence, in which possibilities *are* inherent.

Against the background of this philosophical discourse, Osborne formulates his criticism of Koselleck. The German historian refers to the difference between 'experience' and 'expectation', a gap that arose during modernity, and, in retrospect, in history in general as a result of the modern understanding of time. It has led to the fact that possibilities are produced at the cost of passing reality. But according to Osborne, Koselleck has not sufficiently thought through the dialectics between 'experience' and 'expectation'. This is also true of the way in which the 'historical understanding of time' is determined by the historical development of capitalism and communism. Using the collapse of communism in Eastern Europe and the Twin Towers as examples, Osborne demonstrates that Koselleck's concept of horizon lacks the *un*expected, as formulated in Heidegger's *Vorlaufigkeit*, and the *in*determined (Husserl's '*in*determinateness'). And thus, concludes Osborne, it is precisely thanks to this unexpected aspect, which we also encounter in contemporary experimental art practices, that punctures can be made in the 'horizons of expectation'.

How these punctures can be visualized is explained by Hito Steyerl in her paper 'In Free Fall: A Thought Experiment'. Whereas the majority of contributions in *On Horizons* focus on the philosophical context

of the concept of horizon and its political applications and implications, Steyerl brings up its art historical employment. A horizon suggests stability; it defines the boundaries of communication and understanding. Beyond the horizon is muteness and silence. In painting, the surveyable, calculable, homogenous space, and therefore the linear, predictable notion of time, was represented by means of central perspective. In J.M.W. Turner's paintings, and later on in futuristic works, that unity was undermined. In contemporary representations, a vertical perspective is increasingly being used, or the perspective of the absent pilot, as Steyerl says. Precisely where, for example, is the perspective in James Cameron's film *Avatar* (2009)? In this and other contemporary works, the solid ground beneath our feet turns out to be extremely fragile and fragmented. We are transformed into hypothetically floating viewers. Actually, suggests Steyerl, we are even in a continual freefall. In the new visualizations, we are flooded with a dislocating, disorientating gaze. This creates artistic possibilities. The perspective of the freefall forces us to reconsider verticality as a social theme – and to rise in action against the difference between above and under, rich and poor.

Thanks to this and other inspiring contributions and to careful editing, *On Horizons* makes for hard-to-put-down reading. In these turbulent times on the economic and political fronts, both nationally and internationally, the book formulates, contextualizes and conceptualizes possibilities for artistic projects. Eventual difficulties and pitfalls are pointed out by T.J. Demos and others. In general, the authors seem to have maintained a positive tone in their essays. The word 'hope' is even mentioned. Could a new interpretation of the concept of 'horizon' actually have been found in the BAK's critical reader?

Josephine Bosma, *Nettitudes: Let's Talk Net Art*

Eric Kluitenberg

Rotterdam, NAi Publishers, ISBN 978-90-5662-800-0, 272 p., € 23.50

Nettitudes, the new book by Josephine Bosma, is an important contribution to the often confusing and unbalanced discussion about the Internet and contemporary art. This contribution becomes especially clear from what the book does not do. First of all, Bosma does not try to offer a historical overview of the phenomenon that she calls 'net art'. She also indicates clearly why it is difficult to mark out this area unequivocally, for there are widely differing views as to how the interaction between the Internet and contemporary art should be interpreted. Indeed, net art must in the first place be seen in a broader context than that of contemporary art, because the development of this 'genre' cannot be seen separately from the various forms of network culture with which it sometimes partly converges or by

which it is influenced.

Moreover, Bosma does not wish to call net art a discipline or movement, as the entire terrain is too diverse and heterogeneous for that, and also has too much of a cross-disciplinary character. Nor is it a good idea to have net art purely coincide with the medium of the Internet, which itself can hardly be described. When the same problem is approached from an art theoretical point of view, limiting net art to a particular medium is also absolutely absurd. Bosma herself refers to Rosalind Krauss, the American art theorist, who in her famous essay 'Sculpture in the Expanded Field' argued that contemporary art has wrested itself from the yoke of the medium – it has entered an 'expanded field' in which every material or medium can be appropriated, but to which the

'work' can never be reduced.

That does not mean that the medium as a category can simply be shoved aside. This would lead to a simplistic dichotomy between conceptualism versus materialism – a false contradiction, according to Bosma, which would only work counter-productively in trying to better understand the phenomenon she investigates. What is of primary importance for most of the works that fall under the term 'net art' is a good understanding of the network culture from which they spring: the interactions that artists have online with one another and with the public. Bosma furthermore points out that net art does not only refer to art that takes place in one way or another on the Internet and on the screen. It can also concern work that is directly inspired by the new realities that the Internet and online cultures create, but whose manifestation takes place entirely off-line, separately from the Internet.

Therefore, the definition she uses to describe net art reads in its shortest form as: art that is rooted in or based on Internet cultures. This way, she prevents an arbitrary broadening of the concept, for only works which cannot be seen separately from the cultures that have developed around the Internet can legitimately be considered net art. With this definition, it is clear that the phenomenology, logic and structure of the Internet cannot be bypassed when coming up with an adequate description of net art. No more than can net art be reduced to a technological genre.

According to Bosma, it is hard to give a good description of this heterogeneous and cross-disciplinary field and introduce some structure into the discussion, but not impossible. In order to get a grasp of the material, she introduces five key concepts by which the vast majority of the works that she calls net art can be understood: Code / Flow / Screen / Matter / Context.

She uses 'Code' to look at work that primarily is aimed at the technical infrastructure and software that form the underpinnings of the Internet. This is the most abstract category, accounting for the fact that the Internet in fact rests upon a series of agreements set down in technical protocols. The fact that interesting artistic experiments are being carried out in precisely this inaccessible area indicates the depth of the artistic research behind those experiments. Bosma unlocks this hermetic area with a clear description of the classical project 'Web Stalker' by the British artist collective I/O/D.

'Flow' refers to the remote connections that are made through the Internet, with the emphasis on live performance and network installation art. While distance and spatial relations do not vanish in the digital network, the spatial logic and the forms of exchange (image, sound, information) that can take place in the new spatial configurations do change radically. These processes are manifested by the performative aspect, particularly live performance.

'Screen' refers to the complex (technological) processes behind the fragile visual form of net art works. In these works, the semblance of a stable image is often undermined by the underlying process. Interaction with this type of work makes the viewer aware of the capacity of endless transformation that characterizes the digital image.

'Matter' investigates the role that the hardware, the physical machinery behind the 'immaterial' network, plays in net art – sometimes by literally putting these machines on stage, sometimes also by presenting absurd or faulty machinery.

Finally, 'Context' is about the social and political context in which a certain category of net art works chooses an articulated position. Particularly this category of works been given a lot of attention by critics over the course of the years, but according to Bosma it is by no means representative of the entire field of net art.

Nettitudes is divided into two sections. The first section frameworks the discussion on net art, gives definitions and discusses the positions of other theorists and art critics, such as Tilman Baumgärtel, Julian Stallabras and Rachel Green. Here, Bosma also introduces the concepts mentioned above in order to provide some structure and orientation for the discussion on net art. In the second section, she examines the various positions taken by artists and movements in network culture over the years. Then she goes into the thorny debate on the conservation of net art works. The book closes with a chapter on Internet-related sound art, a form that adds an 'intimate' dimension of its own to net art.

Nettitudes is a breath of fresh air. An important and under-exposed artistic genre is finally getting the serious attention it deserves. *Nettitudes* also offers a useful analysis for the further development of a critical and sound substantive 'discourse' on the exchange between the Internet and the production and reception of contemporary art.

Jeroen Boomgaard, *Wild Park: Het onverwachte als opdracht*

Amsterdam, Fonds BKVB, 2011, ISBN 978-90-76936-00-0, 98 p., € 15.-

Maaike Lauwaert

The sixth essay published by the Netherlands Foundation for Visual Arts, Design and Architecture (Fonds BKVB), titled *Wild Park: Het onverwachte als opdracht* (Wild Park: The Unexpected as Commission) and written by Jeroen Boomgaard, expounds upon the thorny subject of art in public space. Thorny because art in public space is marked by constantly changing administrations, conventions and ideas regarding its role and function. This has not always led to the best art, and certainly not to a cohesive collection. The eclectic and heterogeneous quantity of sculpture in the Netherlands is overwhelming and often difficult to interpret.

By means of three major questions – where, who and why – Boomgaard guides us through this complex field. The first question looks at the place where art in public space is located, the second scrutinizes the public itself, and the third concerns the role, function and significance of art in public space.

The essay begins, however, with an introductory chapter on animal figures in public space. Nowadays we see more animal than human representations; they are more neutral than people and unlike modernist art, for example, have no programme or agenda. When clear, collective ideals cannot be expressed, animals are an easy solution because of their 'empty anecdotic' nature. Animals in public space reflect a postmodernist avoidance of meaning and, caught between the divergent interests of commissioners and makers, they constitute an escapist gesture. This gesture can generate unexpected meanings.

The 'where' of art in public space is a complex question. The public nature of what we once called 'public space' is steadily diminishing and is increasingly being surveyed, privatized and commercialized. Because the public nature of space is becoming blurry, we have more need to make it concrete: to transform the undefined space into a defined place. Converting space into place, or 'solidifying' as Boomgaard also calls it, can, for instance, be done through the installation of a work of art. What's more, this is also a way for power to manifest itself, to claim a place, a restructuring project, new building or construction site. The making of such a claim used to be easier than it is now: the ruler was simply put on a pedestal. Nowadays we are confronted with a complex, composite power of government, public and private parties. The democratic exercise of power has led in the worst cases to compromise art (the result of the consensus machine) or meteor art (which lands on earth out of nowhere). But there are also good examples of works that function as unreliable signals of power, as jammers. This, according to Boomgaard, is the most important task of art in public space and also the reason why commissioners are fond of roundabouts, for these places, after all, strip the works quickly and efficiently of their power.

All the same, wherever sculptures end up, they are seen by people. That seeing is not always on purpose, often it's accidental and sometimes even unwanted. The audience for art in public space is '*always* present and *never* demonstrable'. That makes it an ungrateful audience and an uncertain factor that is difficult to allow for. Community art attempts to calculate in this uncertain factor through the active participation of the public. Since the mid-1990s, participation projects have been launched as a palliative for disrupted districts, alienated population groups and painful rebuilding trajectories. This has led to 'an overwhelming amount of depressing participation art', but also to successful projects that manage to avoid the paradox of the invisible audience and find a balance between too little and too much participation. Boomgaard concludes by stating that the elitist, educative perspective in which art is served to public space like cod liver oil for a healthy social body is no longer the norm. But then, what purpose does art in public space serve?

It has already been mentioned that the complex democratic exercise of power has produced a great diversity of art in public space. An unequivocal demonstration of power is thus no longer the primary function of art in public space. Boomgaard argues that the quality of a work can be measured by how it deals with the entirety of expectations, requirements and possibilities, rather than its aesthetics or its success with the public. The challenge is to keep autonomy and engagement in balance, not to unintentionally introduce new forms of disciplining, not to accidentally serve things that you wanted to oppose or that are not worth serving, to question both the economic model and art's place in the public arena. No easy task. And yet sometimes it's possible to realize work that is critical, ambiguous and unexpected. That can only happen 'when all dominant codes of amusement, brightening up, improvement, emancipation, branding, cohesion and identity forming are carefully avoided or played out against one another. Then the unexpected has a chance.'

For Boomgaard, works of art in public space are a kind of mirror of the health of our democracy. 'A poorly functioning democracy brings forth bloodless images commissioned by leaders who do not want to take any responsibility for their lack of ideas and pass the buck to citizens in a half-hearted attempt at participation without any real chance for change.' Strong works, on the other hand, 'show a government that is prepared to offer space to deviation and experiment and that considers precisely that space to be the representation of its presence'. This last observation has a sharp edge to it, which Boomgaard does not directly address. For we can ask ourselves whether giving room to the unexpected isn't in essence a sly tactic of annexing, whereby enemies and fault finders become part of the system. This paralyses truly critical potential, undermining its power and rendering it harmless. Expect the unexpected, that's the paradox.

Boomgaard succeeds in feeling out the major questions, the core themes and problems of art in public space in a lucid and sharp manner. He offers handholds for weighing art in public space, for making better policy for this complex field, and for skirting dangers for commissioners as well as artists. This is a philosophical book with a practical sensitivity, that by way of art in public space interrogates the place of art in our society and the state of our democracy.

Jeroen Boomgaard is lector for Art and the Public Domain at the Gerrit Rietveld Academy in Amsterdam and also heads up the Master's Artistic Research programme at the University of Amsterdam. In 2011, he published *Wild Park. Het onverwachte als opdracht*.

Heath Bunting is a computer artist and co-founder of net.art. He is banned for life from the USA because of his anti-genetic work. Currently he is producing an expert system for identity mutation.

Jodi Dean teaches political theory at Hobart and William Smith Colleges in Geneva, New York. As author or editor, she has published ten books, including *Democracy and Other Neoliberal Fantasies* (2009) and *Blog Theory* (2010). She co-edits *Theory & Event*, an international journal of contemporary ideas.

Zachary Formwalt is an artist and filmmaker based in Amsterdam. His work has been shown at, among other places, Kunsthalle Basel, Wexner Center for the Arts, Stedelijk Museum Amsterdam, and Casco – Office for Art Design and Theory in Utrecht.

Roel Griffioen studied art history and journalism and is now doing the research master Visual Arts, Media & Architecture at VU University Amsterdam. He regularly publishes texts on architecture and public space. A previous article on the ideal of transparency appeared in the magazine *Kunstlicht*, of which he is editor.

Boris Groys is since 2009 a Full Professor of Russian and Slavic Studies at New York University, New York. As of December 2009, he is also a Senior Research Fellow at the Academy of Design in Karlsruhe, Germany. He additionally curates various exhibitions and publishes articles and books, including *Art Power* (2008) and *Going Public* (2010). Appearing in 2012: *Introduction to Antiphilosophy*.

Eric Kluitenberg is an independent theorist, writer and curator who focuses on culture, media and technology. He was head of the media programme of De Balie, centre for culture and politics in Amsterdam, and teaches and lectures regularly throughout Europe and beyond. Recent publications include the theme issues 'Hybrid Space' (*Open* no. 11, 2006) and '(Im)Mobility (*Open* no. 21, 2011), of which he was guest editor; *Book of Imaginary Media* (2006) and *Delusive Spaces* (2008).

Maaike Lauwaert obtained her doctorate in cultural sciences and works as a visual art programmer for Stroom Den Haag. Over the last ten years she has published articles on visual art in magazines like *Witte Raaf*, *Metropolis M*, *A Prior*, *mister Motley* and *Tubelight*.

Sven Lütticken teaches art history at VU University Amsterdam. He is the author of *Secret Publicity: Essays on Contemporary Art* (2006) and *Idols of the Market: Modern Iconoclasm and the Fundamentalist Spectacle* (2009). Blog: http://svenlutticken.blogspot.com

Jill Magid seeks intimate relations with impersonal structures. She is intrigued by hidden information, being public as a condition for existence, and intimacy in relation to power and observation. Magid is a visual artist, performer and writer. She lives and works in New York.

Stefan Nowotny is a philosopher based in Vienna. He has published widely, especially on philosophical and political topics and currently mainly works on the research project 'Europe as a Translational Space. The Politics of Heterolinguality' carried out by the eipcp. www.eipcp.net

Merijn Oudenampsen has been doing research since January 2011 on populism and cultural studies as a doctoral student at the University of Tilburg. He was guest editor of the 20th edition of *Open* (2010) on the populist imagination, and regularly writes for books, newspapers and magazines on urban development, art, politics and philosophy.

Ilse van Rijn is an art critic. She is working on her dissertation on 'autonomously published artist's texts'.

Felix Stalder is Lecturer in Digital Culture and Network Theory at the Zurich University of the Arts, where he co-directs the media arts programme. He has written and edited several books, including *Open Cultures and the Nature of Networks* (2005), *Manuel Castells and the Theory of the Network Society* (2006) and *Deep Search: The Politics of Search Beyond Google* (2009). He is also a researcher at the Institute for New Culture Technologies in Vienna and a moderator of the *nettime mailing list*. felix.openflows.com

Willem van Weelden is an Amsterdam-based teacher, lecturer and independent writer on new media culture, media theory and interaction design.

CREDITS

Cover Metahaven

Open Cahier on Art and the Public
Domain
Volume 10 (2011) no. 22

Editors Jorinde Seijdel (editor
in chief), Liesbeth Melis
(final editing)

Advisory council Nicolas Bourriaud,
Brian Holmes, Sven Lütticken and
Gerald Raunig

English copy editor D'Laine Camp

Dutch-English translations Jane
Bemont (book reviews by Ilse van
Rijn, Maaike Lauwaert, Merijn
Oudenampsen, Jeroen Boomgaard, Eric
Kluitenberg); text by Roel Griffioen,
interview by Willem van Weelden);
German-English: Aileen Derieg (text
by Nowotny)

Graphic design Thomas Buxó and
Klaartje van Eijk

Printing and lithography Die Keure,
Brugge

Project coordinator Marieke van
Giersbergen, NAi Publishers

Publisher Eelco van Welie, NAi
Publishers

Open is published twice a year
Open 23 will be published in May
2012

Editorial address
SKOR | Foundation for Art and the
Public Domain
Ruysdaelkade 2
1072 AG Amsterdam
the Netherlands
Tel +31 (0)20 6722525
Fax +31 (0)20 3792809
open@skor.nl
www.opencahier.nl

SUBSCRIPTIONS

Abonnementenland
Postbus 20
1910 AA Uitgeest
the Netherlands
0900-2265263 – € 0,10 per minute)
Fax +31 (0)251 310405
www.aboland.nl.

PRICE PER ISSUE

€ 23.50

SUBSCRIPTION PRICES

(postage included)
the Netherlands: € 32.50
Within Europe: € 39.50
Outside Europe: € 45.00
Students: € 24.50

SUBSCRIPTION CANCELLATION

Cancellations (in writing only) must
be received by Abonnementenland
eight weeks prior to the end of the
subscription period. Subscriptions
not cancelled in time are automati-
cally renewed for one year.

Voor de volledige inhoudsopgave
op auteur, artikel en thema zie:
www.opencahier.nl

open

(IN)SECURITY

(NO) MEMORY

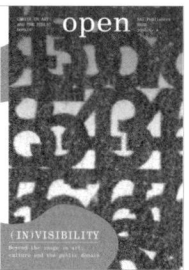

(IN)VISIBILITY

SOUND

(IN)TOLERANCE

HYBRID SPACE

FREEDOM
OF CULTURE

THE RISE OF THE
INFORMAL MEDIA

ART AS
A PUBLIC ISSUE

SOCIAL
ENGINEERING

THE ART BIENNIAL
AS GLOBAL
PHENOMENON

A PRECARIOUS
EXISTENCE

2030: WAR ZONE

BEYOND PRIVACY

THE POPULIST
IMAGINATION

(IM)MOBILITY

NAi Publishers is an internationally orientated publisher specialized in developing, producing and dis-
tributing books on architecture, visual arts and
related disciplines.
www.naipublishers.nl info@naipublishers.nl

It was not possible to find all the copyright holders
of the illustrations used. Interested parties are
requested to contact NAi Publishers, Mauritsweg 23,
3012 JR Rotterdam, the Netherlands.

Available in North, South and Central America through
D.A.P./Distributed Art Publishers Inc, 155 Sixth Ave-
nue 2nd Floor, New York, NY 10013-1507, Tel 212
6271999, Fax 212 6279484.

Available in the United Kingdom and Ireland through
Art Data, 12 Bell Industrial Estate, 50 Cunnington
Street, London W4 5HB, Tel 208 7471061, Fax 208
7422319.

SKOR | Foundation for Art and the Public Domain is an
organization whose objective is to realize special art
projects in public and semi-public settings
www.skor.nl info@skor.nl

Printed and bound in Belgium

ISSN 1570-4181
ISBN 978-90-5662-839-0